In Their Own Words

American Women in World War I

edited by
Elizabeth Foxwell

In Their Own Words: American Women in World War I

Introduction and biographical material copyright © 2015 by Elizabeth Foxwell
First Oconee Spirit paperback printing: September 2015

ISBN 978-0-9859105-7-8

Oconee Spirit Press, Waverly, TN www.oconeespirit.com

Library of Congress Cataloging-in-Publication Data

Foxwell, Elizabeth

In their own words: American women in World War I/ Elizabeth Foxwell

1. World War, 1914-1918 - Personal narratives, American. 2. World War, 1914-1918 – Participation, Female – United States. 3. Women and war – United States.

10 9 8 7 6 5 4 3 2

Printed and bound in the United States. The text paper is SFI certified. The Sustainable Forestry Initiative® program promotes sustainable forest management.

Cover design by Karen Jackson

About the cover. Anna Perit Rochester (later Kennedy) feeds Sergeant W. B. Hyer, Company M, 166th Infantry, 42nd Division at Souilly Evacuation Hospital No. 6 and Evacuation Hospital No. 7, Souilly, Meuse, France, 14 Oct. 1918. Image from Roy Coles Photograph Collection, U.S. Army Heritage and Education Center, Carlisle, PA.

To the American women who served in World War I

"No matter how patriotic or brave were the men or how self-sacrificing, . . .
the women always went them one better."
--General John J. Pershing, May 1922

Table of Contents

A Brief Chronology of World War I

1914

June 28: Archduke Franz Ferdinand assassinated in Sarajevo

July 28: Austria-Hungary declares war on Serbia

Aug. 4: Germany declares war on Belgium

Aug. 10: Great Britain declares war on Germany, France declares war on Austria-Hungary

Aug. 23: Japan declares war on Germany

Aug 30: German air raid on Paris

Sept.: First Battle of the Marne; S.S. *Red Cross* dispatched with medical personnel and supplies

Oct.: First Battle of Ypres

Oct. 31: Japan captures German-held Tsingtao, China

Dec.: Christmas truce, France

1915

Feb.: Germany states that merchant vessels of neutral nations are not immune to sub attacks

Apr./May: Second Battle of Ypres

May 7: German sub sinks the *Lusitania*; 124 Americans are among the nearly 2,000 casualties

May 23: Italy declares war on Austria-Hungary

June: Unsuccessful Gallipoli operation results in approximately 142,000 Allied casualties

July: Germans surrender in South Africa

Oct.: Central Powers forces invade Serbia

1916

Feb.: German offensive at Verdun

Mar. German sub attacks steamer *Essex* with some loss of life; Americans on board

Apr.: Lafayette Escadrille established with American aviators

May: British and French divide up Middle East in secret Sykes-Picot Agreement; Germany halts sub warfare in response to threats by President Woodrow Wilson; German-British Battle of Jutland

June: Arab Revolt begins against the Ottoman Turks, eventually involving Lawrence of Arabia; Battle of the Somme starts

Aug.: Naval Act of 1916 fails to exclude women from serving in the U.S. naval reserve

1917

Jan.: Germany resumes sub attacks

Feb: German sub sinks Cunard liner *Laconia*; two Americans killed

Mar.: Zimmerman telegram reveals German plans for return of AZ, NM, and TX to Mexico; British take Mesopotamia; Russian Revolution begins; the U.S. Navy's Bureau of Navigation tells naval district commanders that they may recruit women for certain positions

Apr. 1: German sub sinks S. S. *Aztec*; 28 Americans die

Apr. 2: President Wilson asks Congress for a declaration of war

Apr. 6: After Senate vote, House votes for US entry into the war. Dissenters include Reps. Jeanette Rankin (R–MT) and Charles Lindbergh Sr. (R–MN).

Apr. 28: Congress passes Selective Draft bill

Apr./May: French soldiers mutiny

May: Germany bombs Britain

June: American troops arrive in France; Espionage Act makes it a crime to convey information that helps the enemy and to subvert the draft

July: Third Battle of Ypres (Passchendaele)

Aug.: German sailors mutiny

Nov.: First American POWs captured by German forces

Dec.: Rep. Murray Hulbert (D–NY) introduces bill to admit women to military service, including the aviation service of the Signal Corps; is unsuccessful; British troops seize Jerusalem from Turks

1918

Mar.: First cases of influenza reported in KS

June: Battle of Belleau Wood

Jul. 15: Killing of Czar Nicholas II and family

Jul./Aug.: Aisne-Marne operation by Allies

Sept.: St. Mihiel operation by Allies

Oct.: Austria and Hungary split; Czechs capture Prague and declare Czechoslovakia an independent nation

Nov. 9: Abdication of Kaiser Wilhelm II

Nov. 10: Abdication of Emperor Karl of Austria

Nov. 11: Armistice signed

1919

Jan.: Opening of Peace Conference at Versailles

"I'm Sure I'll Come Back a Much Better Person":

An Introduction to *In Their Own Words*
Elizabeth Foxwell

I wondered if . . . it would always be necessary to reserve honours
for women till after they are dead.
— *Muriel St. Clair Stobart, Miracles and Adventures (1935)*

Without World War I, I would not be here.

My grandfather, a cook, was in the same regiment as my great-uncle and met the sister of his Army buddy on a visit; they were married in 1922. Called up late in the war, Sam Foxwell and William Becker served in the quartermaster corps at Camps Mills and Upton, and saw their fellow soldiers die in the influenza pandemic.

Although two of my male relatives had such wartime service, my interest in the war takes a direction away from my own family. A devotion to Vera Brittain's *Testament of Youth* led me to other World War I narratives by women, including Joyce Marlow's fine anthology *The Virago Book of Women and the Great War, 1914–18*. But British women tended to predominate in these accounts and, if any American women were represented, they tended to be those in the public eye (for example, Edith Wharton). Books such as Lettie Gavin's *They Also Served: American Women in World War I* paint a broad panorama of involvement by American women, but excerpts restricted by space or what actually exists in the record may leave the reader hungry for more. Frustration can occur when reading these women's obituaries, as they may provide only glancing references to or complete absences in coverage of war service, or offer tantalizing nuggets of experiences that fail to yield a more substantial account in the public record.

There also can be the mistaken impression that, as the U.S. entry into the war did not occur until April 1917, the involvement of U.S. men and women must stem from that date, despite the numbers of American men who joined

Allied forces or the American men and women involved in the Red Cross, the American Field Service, the American Friends Service Committee, the Salvation Army, the Scottish Women's Hospitals, the YMCA, and similar groups. On the American Red Cross Web site, the total number of its American WWI volunteers is stated as 8 million, including nearly 24,000 nurses; its Motor Corps of approximately 12,000 people was composed primarily of women. The Department of Veterans Affairs places the number of female nurses in the Army and Navy at more than 23,000, the number of Navy "yeomanettes" at approximately 12,000, and the number of women in the Marine Corps at 307 (2). It states that 172 women died in the war, with 4 deaths attributed to "enemy action" (1). Scratch below the sterile surface of the list of names, however, and some disturbing stories emerge: the Mare Island yeomanette murdered by her husband on a ferry near San Francisco; the ex-yeomanette who committed suicide in Washington, DC; the two nurses dead in a gun misfire aboard the *S. S. Mongolia*, followed by a congressional inquiry; the canteen worker killed in a German air raid on Paris; scores of victims who perished from influenza and related causes.

Probably the most widespread activity for women in the war was relief work. The Women's Oversea Hospitals USA of the National American Woman Suffrage Association sent 70 American female physicians, nurses, and staff to France. They formed a hospital unit under the auspices of the French government—not the American, as the Medical Reserve Corps of the U.S. Army did not accept women until late in the war (NAWSA 3). In November 1918, it was reported that the American Medical Women's Association had placed 78 volunteer doctors and 28 medical staff in France; established hospitals in France, Greece, and Serbia; and cared for wounded soldiers and their families in the United States ("Jean Eliot's" 15). Their services were especially desired to provide care for Muslim women ("Serbs Call for Women Physicians" 3). In 1920, the YMCA stated that 3,400 women served in its canteens for the American Expeditionary Force in France, with more than 50 who had worked in conditions under fire; one worker, Marion Crandall, died when a shell hit in Ste. Menehould (39–40). It also reported 107 women workers with the YMCA's overseas service to the Navy.

Substantial contributions also were made by alumni from women's colleges such as the 19 women of the Smith College Relief Unit, the 250 women in the Wellesley Unit for War Service in France and other organizations involved in war service, and the 111 women in the Vassar Red Cross and other groups. Approximately 350 women worked for the American Fund for French Wounded and its successor, the reconstruction-oriented American Committee for Devastated France. Enterprising women funded and operated their own initiatives such as Georgianna R. Sheldon and other American residents in Florence, who established the American Hospital for Italian Wounded.

Not all were fans of their presence. Bestselling novelist and trained nurse Mary Roberts Rinehart, who covered the war for the *Saturday Evening Post* and toured military medical facilities in Belgium, England, and the United States, was critical of the numbers of American women overseas, stating in the April 1918 *McClure's* that most were "actually in the way" ("Woman" 56). In January 1918, the Committee on Public Information announced that the State Department was issuing U.S. passports to only those women "imperatively required" in France by a relief agency; "the free lance feminine war worker is now a thing of the past," it asserted, "Government officials having recognized that her presence in the war zone is an embarrassment" ("Passports" 4).

This anthology endeavors to highlight American women's roles in the war through their own accounts produced during and immediately after the war period, thus providing a less constructed and more immediate picture of their participation that is personal and powerful. It seeks to answer questions such as "What did they do? What did they see? What did they think and feel?". To reach beyond the impression that women's role in the war was confined to nursing, it shows the perspectives of those in occupations such as canteen worker, dietitian, driver, entertainer, fingerprint clerk, librarian, occupational therapist, physician, Red Cross searcher, refugee facilitator, reporter, stenographer, and switchboard operator. Attention has been paid to insights from varied theaters of the war as well as different faith traditions (e.g., Catholic, Jewish, evangelical Protestant, Quaker).

However, some caveats need to be stated. It can be difficult to find accounts by women that have not passed through some sort of male filter, and many women may have thought it inappropriate to discuss their service, whether for patriotic reasons or perceptions that women should not put themselves forward given the huge numbers of men doing the fighting and the dying. Expectations regarding women's proper conduct during wartime— sending their men off to war without complaint, writing only cheerful letters to their loved ones in uniform—certainly shaped responses.

Censorship of letters written from overseas meant that correspondents could not share the full range of their experiences, even if they wished to do so. Wrote YMCA canteen worker Emma Young Dickson to her mother from Paris in April 1917, "Apparently all we can talk about in a letter is the weather and the state of our health" (n.p.). A certain amount of flag-waving and racist sentiment can be seen in published accounts of the time. Women from upper-class families had more means than women from less privileged backgrounds to afford (and publicize) their service, although Susan Zeiger notes that the majority of women with the AEF were from the lower middle class and supported themselves (2).

Women were denied many duties because of their gender and race/ethnicity, as seen in the cases of female barnstormers such as Ruth Law who fought to enlist, black female nurses who attempted to volunteer for overseas service and were rebuffed, and the members of the Jewish Welfare League who encountered obstacles when they tried to obtain clearance to travel and so did not sail to France until close to the Armistice. As Secretary of War Newton D. Baker wrote to Rinehart in July 1918, "...we cannot take you as an army nurse because you are married, nor as a civilian worker in the hospitals in France because your boys are in the service. That at any rate, is how the regulations stand at the present time." Prohibitions against women at the front did not insulate them from harm, as seen in cases of serious wounds (such as nurse Beatrice MacDonald losing the sight in one eye from injuries sustained in an air raid) and death (such as Red Cross worker Ruth Landon from a German shell).

Some women were decorated at the time, often by foreign governments. But it did not take long for recognition to fade and the more serious effects of their service to emerge. In 1923, American Legion officials noted that one-fifth of the 30,000 women who had served in the Navy during the war had applied for government relief, and it was believed that many more needed such aid

("Legion Starts Fight for Service Women" 2). In 1925, Women's Overseas League president Mary A. Bogart stated that there were 1,000 disabled female veterans in need of hospital care ("Needy Women Veterans" 4). After Edith Nourse Rogers, a Red Cross worker in WWI France and an advocate for disabled veterans as the first congresswoman elected from New England, inspected 40 veterans' hospitals in 1931, she recommended the establishment of facilities specifically for female veterans ("Homes Are Asked of Hoover for U.S. Women Veterans" 9; "Plan Hospital for War Women" 11). In 1937, Dorothy Frooks, head of the Women World War Veterans, charged that cuts in compensation had placed disabled women veterans in a dire situation (Catton 10).

It is sad that in the centenary of the start of the war, so few remember the stories, the service, and the courage of the American women who served in the war. It is hoped that this anthology may bring renewed appreciation for all that they endured and achieved.

Note: The quote in the introduction title is from canteen worker Emma Young Dickson's April 1918 letter to her mother.

"They Were Greatly Surprised... That the Unit... Was Composed Entirely of Women."

From *Women's Oversea [sic] Hospitals U.S.A.* New York: National American Woman Suffrage Assn,1919, p. 11.

Alice Barlow Brown (1869–1957)

Born in Corry, PA, Alice Barlow married James Robert Brown in Arkansas in 1886 and had a son a year later, but the child died in 1888. She received medical degrees from Hahnemann Medical College (now Drexel University College of Medicine) in 1896 and the College of Physicians and Surgeons of Chicago (now University of Illinois College of Medicine) in 1903. A pediatrics specialist, she first practiced in Chicago, teaching at the College of Physicians and Surgeons, and Buffalo. When she moved to Winnetka, she became the first female physician in that town and a founder of the Winnetka Woman's Club.

Rebuffed because of her gender when she tried to join the army's Medical Reserve Corps in World War I, she turned to addressing the medical needs of civilians in northern France with the help of the residents of Winnetka and the American Fund for French Wounded (see Amy Owen Bradley's account for another look at Barlow Brown). On her return from France in August 1919, she noted in New York's *Evening World* that 60 percent of children in the war zone had tuberculosis.

The doctor next served in Serbia with the American Women's Hospitals of the American Medical Women's Association. She then traveled to China, working in a mission hospital, establishing a rural clinic, and becoming health officer at Yengcheng Women's College. Interned by the Japanese for six months during World War II, she came back to the United States in 1943 and eventually lived in Corpus Christi, TX. A bequest after her death endowed a scholarship for students from Arkansas at the University of the South.

"The City of the Dead"
Letter to the Woman's Committee of the Wilmette Guard
(part of the "Letters from World War I" collection, Wilmette [IL]
Public Library)

80 Rue Stanislaus
Nancy, France
November 25th, 1917

... many things have happened, chief of which is our moving to Nancy, which is much nearer to the six villages in which we are doing dispensary work than Toul. During the past week we have taken care of 300 patients, seeing most of them twice during the week. Tuesdays and Fridays are our heaviest days; on these days we take care of 80 patients, ranging in age from babies of seven weeks to very old people. The diseases are impetigo, scabies, conjunctivities [conjunctivitis] (acute and chronic), ulcer of the cornea, eczema, rheumatism, malnutrition and headaches from sleeping in the caves all night with no ventilation; tuberculosis, tonsilitis, adenitis, etc. When you realize that all the physicians have been militarized for the army and that the civil population has to get on as best it can, you will understand better the situation here. So many children complain of mal a tete [headache] that I inquired into the home conditions and soon found the cause—the constant bombarding and consequent sleeping in caves. Poor childre[n], if a gun goes off while we are talking, one sees them cringe and their eyes stare until all is quiet again. This has been going on for three years. It is a wonder that they look as well as they do.

On Wednesdays and Saturdays we go to a town where we work within a very short distance of the German trenches. At this place we were taken to a building where observations are made, and through the glasses we could see the Germans in the trenches. Here, also, we walked a ways in the French trenches.

On our first visit we had only six patients, chiefly old women. Next time many more, and children. I have two bed cases, one a beautiful young girl that I am hoping to take to the hospital at Toul to be prepared for an operation, for which I would so like to have Dr. [Bertha] Van Hoosen [an obstetrician-gynecologist and first president of the American Medical Women's Association]. After we get the children cared for and the women bolstered up, we will only go once a week. Last night the Secretary-General said that a very important person did not want us to go more than once a week unless it was absolutely necessary, because it was so very dangerous. Yet, there are many, many people here who are taking that risk. Between our visits a bomb was dropped that killed four people. It take us nearly an hour to drive to our work. It is through a most beautiful country. The road is camouflaged—that is, material the color of dust is arranged so as to obscure the vision of the road from the aeroplanes. Our host arranged a concert for us, forty boys played and one sang Carmen so beautifully and through it all we heard the [illegible]. Oh yes, when we go to this town we wear gas masks all ready to apply if occasion demands. The faces of these poor people have changed in expression since our visits. They say not only has

America come to their aid in the war, but she has sent her women to help the civilian population.

We are still working under difficulties, as we have to carry all our supplies with us, and my instruments are still in Paris waiting to be brought down in the camion [truck]. The French Government made some new regulations about women driving in the military zone, which has kept our machine in Paris. There are some changes being made in there, because the work has grown so.

Dr. [Julius Parker] Sedgwick [from University of Minnesota] leaves for America December 1st and Dr. [J. H. Mason] Knox [Jr.] of Baltimore . . . is going to have charge of the Meurthe et Moselle district. He came on an inspection tour last week.

We start out at 8 o'clock every morning and work until five just as hard as we can. Mme. [Helene] Delebecque [a Belgian-born woman from Winnetka serving as translator] is indispensable at all times. At Toul one evening she entertained some of the people with a monologue of Dr. Brown doing her dispensary work, using a few French phrases which I have acquired. She certainly is fine, as is also my nurse and my chauffeur. The latter part of this week I have had Mr. Arthur Aldis' [a Chicago realtor and investor] niece, a Miss [Amy Owen] Bradley, take me around. She takes the [names?] of the patients and makes out their record cards, which helps me very much.

On Sunday, November 17th, we had a baptismal service for my two French babies. Mme. Delebecque and I were godmothers. It was an impressive service and both children behaved well. Mine is Paul Joffre Chanal, the other Helen Marguerite Levy, for Mme. Delebecque.

At present were are using the car of the American Fund for French Wounded and could not possibly do the work without it. We are anxiously looking forward to having our own. You know we cannot budge without our military papers—a red book with our birthplace, age, name, etc., also a blue paper allowing one to travel in an automobile.

My gas has gone out and I am finishing my letter by candle light.

Elizabeth Foxwell

From "Dr. Brown Will See France from Plane"
The Lake Shore News (Wilmette, IL) 17 Jan. 1918: 1, 6

80 Rue Stanislas, Nancy
Meurthe et Moselle, France
Dec. 5, 1917

My dear family:

This is a beautifully clear, sunny morning, just such a one as you are having, without snow. Sunday is our day of rest, that is, mending and doing the odd jobs that we have not had time for during the week. Mme. and Miss Van Aken have gone out to do a little shopping, the stores are all open until noon on Sundays which helps us out considerably. I made the breakfast this morning using the last of the coffee I brought with me. I stewed some apples for sauce and made toast on the top of the stove. It was all good. We get a pint of milk daily, boil it and have cafe au lait. During the week we eat an egg for breakfast but as they are ten cents apiece we do not on Sundays. After the twentieth of the month we will go on bread ration as well as sugar. We have not secured our sugar card yet because we have been using our own sugar that I brought with me.

We do not know whether we will remain permanently in these rooms or not. If it will be difficult to buy wood we will go to a hotel, it will be warm there but many things will not be so agreeable as here; the girls are eager to go but I am not.

Friday afternoon when we were at one of our clinics the Secretary-General called to see our rooms to assure himself that we were comfortable. He had a trip last Wednesday in an aeroplane, he said some day he would arrange it so that we could go up in one. Can you imagine it!

This past week has been such an eventful one I scarcely know where to begin. First, we have secured our permanent homes for the dispensaries in two towns, Pompey and Frouard, we begin the work in them Dec. 15, over the doors will be the sign that shows Winnetka is the donor. We get both places for 30 francs a month, and coal furnished by the usine [power plant]; it is their contribution to our good work. The Secretary-General is having them put in order and sends us table, chairs, wardrobe, etc. It is at Frouard that I want to keep two people and have a small maternity hospital. In these two towns are 2,000 people who have had no medical assistance whatsoever, and who will need the frequent visits of a nurse. There is so much needed help to improve the sanitation. The mothers work in the usine, the children do the best they can, the fathers are militarized or killed. One little girl that came to the clinic last Friday when I questioned her about the home conditions, broke down and cried—her mother was killed by a German bomb at Pont-a-Mousson—her father and sister wounded. This week I am going to take her to the children's hospital at Toul as she has heart trouble and needs building up. We are planning a Christmas tree for all the children, 265, in our various clinics.

11:45. The siren is ringing, to the cave I must go—I hear the guns going—after looking out I decided to take a chance—that is what we Americans are apt to do—but the cave is so dark and chilly and I am not dressed. Last Wednesday the Germans sent gas bombs where our boys were in the trenches, in one small town 25 were killed instantly and more were crippled by continual coughing. We wear our masks over our shoulders Wednesday and Saturday, for on these days we work within 20 metres of the German trenches. Yesterday I did my first operation, while doing so the guns were firing continually, they say that this town will be absolutely riddled by the German guns. It has been a beautiful town, but now it makes one think of the city of the dead!

There are several small towns adjoining where there is still quite a large civilian population; in these towns I learned that my coming had been announced by the town crier. M. [Léon] Mirman is so overjoyed with our work and its results that he wants everyone to take advantage of it. Yesterday he insisted [on] taking me to one of the towns to show me off! I called on two old ladies who are very ill; one, 90 years old who is dying, the other 72.

Everyone here with a nice home has stowed away their paintings and furniture and gone to the south of France, leaving only caretakers to look after things. It takes us an hour to drive to this town and since we began our work many changes have occurred. The road is a constant stream of moving troops—the country is so beautiful—some portions look like California—last Tuesday a light snow fell which made the mountains stand out in a bright, clear outline.

Thursday was St. Nicholas Day—the patron saint of Lorraine—a day celebrated as we do Christmas. We were invited to lunch with Mme. Jalard of

Champigueulle[s]. We have a clinic at C——— every Monday and Thursday mornings. The Jalards have a beautiful home surrounded by four acres of ground, everything we had for luncheon was raised on the place. There was a very distinguished guest asked to meet us, a Captain B———, later a lieutenant, who is one of the General's aid[e]s came bringing the General's compliments and gratitude for the wonderful work we are doing for the civil population. The captain has asked us to visit his camp next Sunday at D———, he is to have some music for us. The lieutenant invited us to a theater party on the twenty-third—the soldiers are to give it, we go with the Jalards. Mme. Jalard has been so kind, it was she who put the flowers in the dispensary on our arrival. She has three children: a son 18, one 11, and a little girl of six. Her home has been the home of so many officers and men since the war began she has many souvenirs, autographs, cartoons of all the phases of life pertaining to the war, post-cards, etc. She has lost two fine-looking brothers in the war.

The Secretary-General is having a man look for a furnished apartment for us—then we will have a servant and keep house—that is, if we can get coal and wood. General Pershing has sent out a warning to all Americans in France to economize on fuel and gasoline. We keep our sitting room at 60 and my bedroom is at 40, so you see we are getting accustomed to the cold temperature that the French endure. ...

Amy Owen Bradley (Suter) (1893-1939)

Born in Milton, MA, Amy Owen Bradley was one of five surviving children of Richards Merry Bradley and his wife, artist Amy Aldis Bradley. Bradley's father had a real estate firm in Boston, and she graduated from the Winsor School in Brookline. Along with other Winsor alumni, Bradley served as a motor driver for the American Fund for French Wounded, an organization cofounded by Anne Tracy Morgan (daughter of J. P. Morgan) and Isabel Stevens Lathrop to supply French hospitals and provide aid parcels to wounded servicemen. A collection of Bradley's letters home was published as *Back of the Front in France* (1918). In August 1920, she married Philip Hales Suter, a Harvard graduate who worked for the American Field Service during the war and later the investment firm Spencer Trask; they had three children.

"The Enemy Is Coming for You"
From *Back of the Front in France* (1918): 87–93

Nancy, November 25, 1917

. . . For the last four days I have been driving Dr. Alice Brown [Alice Barlow Brown; see Barlow Brown entry], of Winetka [sic], Ill., on her rounds of dispensary work. She visits six towns, each twice a week, to look after the women and children, who have had no medical care since the war. Dr. Brown doesn't speak a word of French, but she is so gentle and sweet with the people that they have absolute trust in her, and no matter how much she hurts them, in treating infected fingers, pricking boils etc., they always thank her, sometimes with tears in their eyes.

As helpers she has a trained nurse and Madame [Helene] Delabeck [Delebecque], a Belgian, who has a coiffeur establishment in Winetka. Madame Delabeck is a wonder, and knows just how to explain to the people what they must do to cure themselves, and knows too just when to laugh, and when to sympathize with their ailments.

In the dispensary we have happenings from the tragic to the ridiculous every day; for instance, at the end of the day, the nurse is cleaning a child's head with strong antiseptic, Madame Delabeck is tactfully telling a mother that she must wash her baby, while I flash the pocket flash light (no other light being allowed on account of the nearness of the Boche) down a small boy's throat for Dr. Brown, at the same time coaxing him to put out his tongue—"tire la langue, mon petit." His proud mamma stands by, blandly smiling at her prodigy's tongue prowess. All of a sudden Dr. Brown sees four small boys in the background, who, not wishing to be outdone, stick out their tongues, while one of them is about to cast her only thermometer on the floor! Consternation, but helplessness on her part because she can't speak French. Finally, however, the thermometer is rescued, the right tongue is waving in the air, the others restored to their proper places and the consultation continues.

I wish I could keep on with this work as it is the kind I like best.

The sickness among the people here is due mostly to two things: —nerves from being constantly bombed and living in cellars, and bad nourishment. Nearly every child that comes in is suffering from the food, and many of the grown people too.

The war bread here is very bad, and has made a good many people ill, including myself, and we ourselves have had practically to give up eating it.

The children have a fearful amount of impetigo [a contagious skin infection] and scabies, they nearly all have worms, due, Dr. Brown thinks, to the bad lard; pink-eye and bad colds are ever present, and in one place they have mumps. The grown people suffer more from nerves, which affect the digestion, and give them headaches and bad eyes.

The husbands of many of these women have been killed or wounded; the women have to go out to work, and leave their once tidy homes neglected and dirty.

All of these towns, except one, contain factories where the women are employed and which are constantly bombed.

Imagine the strain of working from 6 a.m to 6 p.m.,—knowing that the blast furnaces light up the sky for miles around, hearing the alarm for an air raid go off, keeping on working, though you know that the enemy is coming for you.—then on top of that having your husband at war, and your children, sometimes little ones, running the streets all day with no lunch except a piece of war bread and a bit of chocolate because there isn't time to go home and cook for them. That is how they have lived for the last three years. Do you wonder that they sometimes come to us and say: "I don't know what the matter is, but I seem to feel tired all the time." Yet these women are the very ones who want to fight the war until there is a deciding victory for France, and I have never heard them complaining of their hardships. Sometimes they sigh and comment on the length of the war,—all are weary of it but usually they say: "We shall hold out to the very end." They have absolute faith and trust in us and in the English, of whom they say: "Ils ne lâcheront jamais" ("they will never let go"). They wait four hours to see "la doctoresse Américaine" and so many flock to her that we have to turn some away. The very fact that we are helping the civilians makes them think that we must have immense resources ready at hand. We are the only Americans they have seen, and they are so grateful and eager that it is pathetic to see them and almost frightening to realize the faith they have in us to end the war, and start them on a normal existence again. I pray we may not fail them when they need us most!

Gladys Cromwell (1887–1919)

Gladys Cromwell, second from left in hat, and Dorothea Cromwell, far right, with other American Red Cross workers at a Red Cross canteen in Souilly, France. (Anna Perit Rochester, on cover, is on the far left). Library of Congress, Prints and Photographs

Poet Gladys Cromwell was a daughter of Frederic Cromwell, president of the Mutual Life Insurance Co, and sister of Seymour Cromwell, a president of the New York Stock Exchange. She volunteered with her twin sister, Dorothea, for YMCA canteen service in France in 1918, working in Chalon-sur-Marne and Souilly and reported to be constantly under bombardment. As they were sailing for home in January 1919, the sisters committed suicide by jumping off the S. S. *La Lorraine.* Accounts indicate that they were exhausted and depressed from the considerable stresses of their service. Novelist Gertrude Atherton, who was on board, provided one account; Bryn Mawr alumnus Margaret Hall, who had served with them, noted that they had been deeply affected by the constant bombing and added, "Supersensitive people should not come here" (Higonnet 140). The French government decorated the sisters posthumously.

An odd coda is the family "jinx" posited in a 1939 *Milwaukee News-Sentinel* article that mentioned that Seymour died in a fall from his horse in September 1925 (Paul 5C). Most strangely, the Cromwells' cousin, Elizabeth, died when she fell—like the sisters—from the liner *Veendam* in June 1925 ("Junior League Girl").

Realization
(from *Poems*, 1919)

There is one syllable that stirs me: War!
I picture what the mortal strife must be
Of Nations clad in youth and bravery.
I hear the voice of human anguish more
Compelling than it ever was before.
Across the universe, beyond the sea,
New life is spilled into infinity,
And the waves tell it moaning on our shore.
How comes it bleaker sorrow I can bear;
The combat sharply drawn, a street, a square
Away? The souls intrenched in frigid line
To fight for purposes no kings define; —
For purposes as grim to them as life?
God, let me apprehend this nearer strife!

"I Rejoice That I Am Here"

As reported in the August 1917 *War Library Bulletin* of the American Library Association, Raymond Fosdick, chair of the War Department's Commission on Training Camp Activities, stated in a June 28, 1917, letter to Librarian of Congress Herbert Putnam that the commission wished to ask the ALA "to assume responsibility for providing adequate library facilities in the thirty-two cantonments and National Guard training camps" (2). By the time of the ALA's June 1918 *War Library Bulletin,* the war library service had established 41 libraries in large camps, 237 libraries in small camps, 249 libraries on naval stations and vessels, and 1,323 libraries in YMCA and Knights of Columbus facilities, as well as sent books to 91 hospitals and Red Cross facilities. This account stated that 385,310 books had been shipped overseas, 411,505 mostly technical books had been bought, and 2.1 million gift books were in use.

It also reported that there were 212 librarians in the war library service; a look at the rosters of names reveals that some 24 percent were women. One of them was Annie S. Cutter, aunt of writer-aviator Anne Morrow Lindbergh. In their work, the librarians encountered servicemen who were trying to plan for a postwar occupation, those who were illiterate, and those who were foreign-born and wished to work on their English or read books in their native language.

Katherine Tappert (Willis) (1883–1979)

Born in Fairfield, IA, Katherine Tappert graduated from Parsons College (IA) in 1905 and the Pratt Institute (NY) in 1911. During World War I, she was the hospital librarian at Camp Upton in New York. She subsequently wrote reviews for *Library Journal* and served as librarian of the *New York Evening Post,* head librarian at the Morristown (NJ) Library, and librarian of the Westchester Library Association (White Plains, NY). In June 1927, she married former textile merchant Grinnell Willis, a son of poet-editor Nathaniel Parker Willis.

"Nothing Is Too Good for Them"

Letter from Katherine Tappert to Julia Robinson, secretary of the Iowa Library Commission, *Iowa Library Quarterly,* Apr.-May-Jun. 1918, 107–08

Base Hospital Library,
U.S., Camp Upton, New York
3 June, 1918

My dear Miss Robinson:

The Base Hospital at Camp Upton is two miles from the camp itself so even though a very good road connects the two places, the hospital is more or less a community in itself. There are now eleven hundred beds and, under construction, convalescent houses that will make room for six hundred more. The medical detachment numbers six hundred, the nursing corps between one hundred and fifty and two hundred and there are more than one hundred officers on the medical staff. This gives you an idea of the size of the community.

The Atlantic division of the Red Cross has built Convalescent Houses for several of the Government Hospitals in its division and it is in this building at Upton that the main library of the hospital is housed. There are shelves for three thousand books in the ingle nooks at the fireplace and since the room is open to the convalescent patients until four in the afternoon and to the men of the medical corps from four until ten, these books are used just as the books of any public library would be.

It naturally would seem that a hospital library would be carried on for the patients of the hospital, and of course, such is the case, but it is impossible to work one week in a base hospital without being impressed with the importance of the work with the medical corps and the influence that it has on the spirit of the hospital. At Upton, the corps is most interesting, six hundred men—many of them young scientists—many of them anything but that—many of them glad that they are doing hospital work and many of them longing for machine guns or airplanes, or the sea—and most all of them longing for overseas duty, which will come late, if at all. There are among them men from all of the universities of our country and many from foreign ones. There are artists, journalists, and musicians and plumbers and electricians and mechanics. And all of these men are doing a hard and useful but more or less thankless work and one that attracts no attention in the great game that is being played.

I have an idea that nothing is too good for them as I have watched the great eagerness with which they have come to the library and asked if it were possible to get, at last, a book that they have longed for. These men for the most part work twelve hours a day and have little time to go to the Camp for any sort of recreation. One man is reading now all of the lives of Oliver Cromwell that I can get for him. Another is reading [Henry Thomas] Buckle's History of England and all of those who read at all follow with the greatest spirit the news from the front as told by the heroes Pat O'Brien, [R. Hugh] Knyvett, [A. J.] Dawson and [Harold R.] Peat. It is impossible to supply the demand for these books for many of them must go into the contagion and infection wards where they are read for two weeks, maybe, and then burned.

The men who are ill are for the most part eager to read of the real thing for most of them are from regiments that are almost ready to embark or from those that are already overseas and they too are impatient to be sent to join their comrades.

The only class of patients that are [*sic*] not keen for "war literature" are those in the psychiatric wards. Since many of these cases are either conscientious objectors or simply abnormal fear cases this is not surprising. The work with these men is very interesting but has to be done very carefully.

I had a pathetic request for Canada Blackie [a prisoner in Sing Sing whose case rallied those interested in prison reform] from a man who had such a record that the ward surgeon thought it quite inadvisable to give him anything that pertained to such experiences. We persuaded him to read the thing that next appealed to him, which was the poetry of [James Whitcomb] Riley and [Eugene] Field. Humor is essential for the men who cannot leave their beds.

The experiences of a day in the wards are endless and I could go on telling you of the individuals whom I meet and the revelations that are made.

After all, the men are just the men that we all know and they read the things that we all read, and think of the things that we all think of and in much the same way. The one thing that I cannot lose sight of is the fact that they cannot go after the thing that they want and what is not brought to them is never theirs.

There are bookshelves in the post exchange and the books here reach a few men who do not come to the Convalescent House. There is a library in the

Officers' House and another in the Nurses' Quarters and each of the barracks in which the medical corps live has its small collection. For the casual reader these do very well but the man be he sick or well, who is really reading for more than the passing of time[,] is always glad to talk of books with the librarian on her rounds or at her desk.

Miriam E. Carey (1858–1937)

A pioneer in libraries for prisons, charitable institutions, and facilities for the mentally ill, Miriam E. Carey was educated at Rockford Seminary (Rockford, IL), Oberlin College, and University of Illinois. She was appointed as supervising librarian for Iowa's board of control for prisons in 1907. In 1909 she became the organizer of the Minnesota State Library Commission.

"A Change of Environment for the Convalescent Soldiers"
Letter from Miriam E. Carey, director, Hospital Library Service, Southern Division, to Julia Robinson, secretary of the Iowa Library Commission
Iowa Library Quarterly, Apr.-May-Jun. 1918, 87–88

Red Cross House
Base Hospital
Camp Gordon, GA
May 31, 1918

My dear Miss Robinson:

Your kind suggestion that I write a few lines about my work finds me at a moment when I can respond though in very informal fashion, as you will see.

Red Cross House at Base Hospital, Camp Gordon has been my field of work for two weeks. The building, which is in the form of a cross, stands on a slight rise of ground at the end of the street on which the base hospital borders. It has the distinction of being the only building at Camp Gordon which is painted and its whiteness against the trees which are close by makes a pleasing picture especially as Camp Gordon is like the hippopotamus that the lady had longed to see—it is "plain."

Within the building there is one large and lofty recreation room, one end of which is raised and forms a platform for theatricals, movies, etc., at night and a sun parlor by day. Opening from this room on both sides are small rooms used for administrative purposes. Around the sides of the recreation room there are built-in shelves for the circulating library which is to serve the sick and convalescent men who are not able to get to the camp library. There are shelves in this room for about 1500 books.

The way we get books for these libraries is to look over the volumes which have been blown in by the [book] "drive" and select the ones that we consider the best suited for the men who are to read them. There are many very desirable books obtained in this way and if it were not for the fact that there are so many illiterate men among the soldiers these donated books would be adequate for the recreational side of the library. But the fact is I crave mightily to have some books of the "Every Boys' library—Boy scout edition" or some other first-rate boys' books. No objection to [G. A.] Henty, Oliver Optic [William T. Adams], [John Townsend] Trowbridge, Munrose [possibly Kirk Munroe], [William O.] Stoddard, [James] Otis, [Ralph Henry] Barbour, etc., but it is surprising how few of these authors were "given away" in the recent whirlwind of gifts.

Camp Gordon is such a large place and the base hospital part seems so interminable to a newcomer that it seemed best to begin to push the books around as soon as we had about five hundred on the shelves. This building is not finished nor is it regularly opened to the public, so it has no phone, no auto service, no orderlies, no baskets—not much of anything to serve in book distribution. However, in the army one learns to make things do and to make them go after a fashion. So after blundering around with baskets and bundles of books for two weeks I found today to my satisfaction that I have managed to get in touch with most of the wards in one way and [sic] another. Scrap books are a great help and this hospital has not enough of them at present. We also use postal albums made by pasting postals on both sides of a folded strip of tough Manilla paper the width of a card. Magazines, small books that have good print, pictures such as the Mentor, and publications like the National Geographic, are also very essential. This morning I fixed up three baskets—quite pretty baskets holding about ten medium sized books—four bundles of magazines and scrapbooks, and a bundle of books for a "contagious" ward from which the books could not be returned. Then I proceeded to wait and wait for someone to come along and get the books across from the house to the wards. Ordinarily it is best to take a basket around to the bedsides of the men and let them choose a book from several. That is the way I like to do it best. Sometimes it is best to make a list of the books and send the whole bunch to the ward master to distribute. There are many of the soldiers who like to read and to whom a book is a great comfort. There are others who have not acquired the habit and who are indifferent to what we have to offer.

There are a few foreign born men in this camp who would be glad to read in their own languages. I wish that I had a few books in Italian at present. And I have met one or two Polish soldiers who would be glad of books in their own language as they cannot read English.

In addition to the ward visits there are a good many books taken out by nurses and officers who come here to the Red Cross Building when their days' work is over for a little change and pleasure. While the purpose of the place is especially to supply a change of environment for the convalescent soldiers, it is also possible for the other residents of the camp to enjoy the spacious comfort of the building.

When the service here is thoroughly organized the librarian will be looked on as one of the house staff and will take her full part in entertaining and assisting the soldier who may be in the building. There are large numbers of "steamer chairs" in the room in which the men can recline at their ease. There will be a trained nurse and dietician in residence whose business it will be to prepare lunches and necessary sustenance for those who come here to spend the day. The only persons who will sleep in this house will be the matron, the executive head, the librarian, and the nurse. The men who are not well enough to walk will be wheeled here in chairs as the wards will be connected with this building by a covered passage or "runway" as they call them.

The librarian will have to be a versatile person, able to tell stories, read aloud, and perhaps teach the ABCs, and she will have to have a patriotic spirit which will enable her to help every man whatever his condition or color. She will have to have the spirit of the best nurses who do the most disagreeable things imaginable for these men no matter who they are and consider that they are doing them for Uncle Sam's soldiers. Some of these nurses are the noblest of women. I look at them and listen to them with the deepest respect and admiration.

I believe that this library work in hospitals will prove to be a great relief to the administrative part of the hospital as well as a great source of pleasure to the soldiers. We are having a great opportunity to do our part to win the war and our medium of service is one of the few things which can follow men everywhere and never change in a vital sense.

I think of the pleasant weeks which I might have spent in Iowa City this summer if I hadn't been *drafted* and I feel sorry to have lost such a privilege. But when I think a little longer I rejoice that I am here and I hope that my friends in Iowa will not forget any of us in the service whether we are wearing khaki or not.

Gertrude Thiebaud (McDuff) (1878–1944)

Gertrude Thiebaud graduated from the University of Wisconsin's library school in 1912. She was librarian at the Peru (IN) Public Library when she entered the ALA's war library service in 1918, serving at Walter Reed in Washington, DC. She later became the librarian at the hospital at Fort McHenry in Maryland and at the Patent Office in Washington, DC. In December 1920, she married Russell Hugh McDuff.

"The Whole Splendid Type of Americanhood About Us"
"Work in a Hospital Library" Library Occurrent Oct. 1918: 83–86
(Note: although this piece was published without a byline, Thiebaud is identified in the June 1918 *War Library Bulletin* as the Walter Reed librarian in this period)

Library work at Walter Reed Base Hospital is so intensely interesting and so varied—to give even a birdseye view of our daily round about the the post will mean a lengthy tale. First of all we reached Washington on May 31st, where we reported to the chief of hospital libraries then on duty, Miss Ernestine Rose. Miss Rose has her desk in the center of the Library War Service Headquarters—which by the way is a large room on the main floor of the Congressional Library [Library of Congress]. Such a busy place—the click of many typewriters, the buzz of telephones, the muffled double-quick of rubber-tired messengers, and above all, the busy and businesslike look of owners and desks as we pass along the aisles make us realize we are in close touch with a very real and alive organization. Miss Rose gave us our credentials, instructing us to report to the commanding officer at Walter Reed by nine o'clock on the morning of June 1. This we did, thoroughly enjoying the newness of a military post and the strangeness of army ways. But it must have been amusing to onlookers to see us flounder about before we decided just about where to alight. Our commanding officer, Col. [Albert E.] Truby, gave us a quick survey of library conditions and needs at the post and directed us to the Red Cross Convalescent House where our desk was to be located and we were to be placed in charge of the books already collected by the A.L.A., The Red Cross, Women's Comfort Section of the District, by the Chaplain of the Post, and by the Y. M. C. A.

Walter Reed has an unusually attractive Red Cross House—a building built and tastily furnished by a number of patriotic women who are living in the capital city. There is none of the bleakness or barreness here that you find in many army post buildings. The windows are curtained, grass rugs are on the floor. The most comfortable of wicker chairs and lounges, piled high with warm-colored cushions, are in abundance. Writing desks and tables for games are plentiful. The walls are lined with bookcases, and her eon these shelves we found our library. Everything from everywhere. Eleanor Glynn [sic], Diamond Dick, Dickens, Histories, Shakespeare, Gasoline engines, Spellers, Modern drama are higgly-piggly around about that big long house. No pockets in the books, no book cards, no paste, no pads, no clips, no rubber bands, no desk. Nothing but hundreds and hundreds of boys strolling about in long woolly gray bathrobes and dozens of women in Red Cross bonnets and several men done up in Red Cross and Y.M.C.A. uniforms. Camels, Fatimas and Lucky Strikes puffing the atmosphere in a lovely cozy blue, and player pianos, Grafanolas [a type of phonograph] and Victrolas, vying with one another to be in the lead. But, oh, it was jolly and we liked it even with the thermometer 99 in the shade and our head splitting from the noise and the smoke.

The Y. M. C. A. here is sharing the Red Cross House, so we had two separate collections of books to throw together, really four since the Chaplain has a collection and the Women's Comfort Section had another bunch. Every man about the place and each woman in or near the house, together with all her special friends, had a certain scheme for the arrangement and management of the library. One by one during that dizzy day they came to us with their suggestions. Some of them mighty clever, too. I remember one man wanted to paint different colored stripes along the books—Red for history, yellow for poetry, blue for drama, and so on. Easy then to see a book out of place.

We sent out an S. O. S. call to the L[ibrary]. W[ar] S[ervice]. for supplies and set the patients to work reshelving the books in a rough alphabetical arrangement. Then we pasted and pasted for days and made out book cards and talked to ten dozen boys all at once and checked out books with the other hand—helped find matches for dead pipes—tucked away extra packages of cigarettes—a favorite fountain pen or a sheet of music in our safest drawer until ward hours were called—or helped write letters for some crippled patron or sympathized with this one because of a threatened S. C. D. [Surgeon's Certificate of Disability] or with that one because the mail brought no letters from home—or with another because hospital days had been so long and he was fretting to get back to duty—or frowned a bit on some lad who taken on an a.w.o.l. and was awaiting a guard house sentence—enjoyed the photographs of best girls, whether wife, mother, or sweetheart. All so human and so sweet, and making us love and clinch our faith in the whole splendid type of Americanhood about us.

Then came our ward visiting. First the men just a day out of ether—too drowsy to care to talk but always ready with a smile and a thank-you look in their eyes for a magazine or a scrapbook left by their bedside. In another two or three days these same boys would be calling merrily to us as we entered their ward, our arms loaded down with books, "Any western stories today?" "This way, Miss Librarian." "Say, I want a Rex Beach." "Oh, I've been waiting weeks to get my hands on [Zane Grey's] Wildfire. Gee, this is luck." "All your Jack London gone—say start at this end of the line first when you come again, will you?" "Can't you find me a book by that fellow [James Oliver] Curwood?" "Good, here is a Kipling and an O. Henry." Sometimes there will be a solemn looking chap reach out his hand for Churchill or Wells or Walpole, but generally at this stage of the game the rough and tumble western tale wins the day. Then such a clatter as there is for Popular Mechanics, World's Work, Life, Judge, Puck, Adventure, American, Red Book, and Saturday Evening Post. If our people back home only realized how our plucky lads, spending weary days in these hospitals, long for really new magazines and plenty of them, they certainly would cut out this sending in from all quarters of the globe all the periodicals

31

they have hoarded since the days of Noah. No present day army man wants them any more than the donors do.

But now it has been a week or more since the operating table and the men are still flat on their backs or just able to sit up in bed, and are beginning to want really worthwhile things to read. Here comes our heavy demand. We simply cannot get enough books on automobile gasoline engines, aeroplane engines, searchlights, tanks, trench warfare, military manuals, bacteriologies, chemistries, algebras, geometries, trigonometries, French texts, Mechanical drawing, Structural, Mechanical, and Civil Engineering. The foreign group, Spanish, Italian, Greek, French, ask for easy helps in English, but most of all they like good stories in their own particular language to help them through the long days in bed.

There is a large demand for one-volume U.S. histories and some for French histories. There is a large demand for modern drama, modern poetry: Shakespeare, too, has his devotees. [Omar] Khayyam and [Robert] Service can be placed high in the list of best sellers. The officers call for really good biography and personal accounts of the present war. Funny, but it is true, Harold Bell Wright is more than popular in the officers' pavilion, with Gene Stratton porter [sic] making quite a hit there also.

Up in the Convalescent House the boys clamor for recent magazines and for newspapers from the various larger centers of the country. One little fellow was almost heartbroken because no newspapers from Wheeling, W. Va., ever arrived in our mail sack. If the citizens of our large cities like New York, Boston, Atlanta, Chicago, Cincinnati, St. Paul, Portland, and San Francisco realized how the men enjoy home papers, they would get together and see that every camp and base hospital in the land is supplied with these periodicals now and throughout the war. . . . .

Our library assistants consist of the patients able to aid us and the young women from the Takoma Park Branch of the District of Columbia Library and from the libraries in the city of Washington who volunteer their services. Added to these, we have a number of trained librarians holding Government positions who come out of evenings, Saturday afternoons, and Sundays to help. Two young married women, whose husbands are army officers, come three afternoons a week. These women are not trained librarians, but are willing to help and learn readily. It is rough and tumble work too, for we do all our shelving, carrying books to the wards and back again, emptying big mail sacks filled with Burleson magazines and packages of books ordered to supply the demand for technical, scientific, military, and language calls, packing and unpacking the large baskets filled with books borrowed from the Washington Public Library. But these are war times and no one is looking for dainty jobs, and every member of our staff is eager and willing to do her share of the work.

Almost from the beginning our circulation reached 190 a day and would easily have been more could we count the number of times a book is read before it leaves a ward. It would be the easiest matter in the world to run the circulation up to 800 or 900 a day right now—could we reach more wards in one day and had we a big enough supply of the type of books the men are calling for. That's the rub—how are we to do efficient library work in these posts unless we can give the type of books needed. The nurses too are asking for material along their line of work, and should have it. The Reconstruction instructors buzz around asking for dozens of copies of this and that thing to supplement the courses of study they are giving. The men over in the Barracks cry for military manuals of every description, and so it goes. It's books we need. No question about the demand.

. . . . Altogether, we must have between three thousand and four thousand people at the Post. About seventeen hundred of these are bed patients. Reconstruction work is the specialty of the Post.

Margaret Mayo (1882–1951)

Margaret Mayo with her husband, Edgar Selwyn, ca. 1911. Library of Congress, Prints and Photographs Division, reproduction no. LC-USZ62-98742.

Born Lillian Slatten in Brownsville, Illinois, Margaret Mayo was an actress, screenwriter, and playwright, perhaps best known for the plays "Polly of the Circus" (1907) and "Baby Mine" (1910) as well as her adaptation of Ouida's *Under Two Flags.* Married for 18 years to Edgar Selwyn (a producer who cofounded Goldwyn Pictures), Mayo was a member of the Over There Theatre League, which entertained American troops in France in 1918.

"[P]erfectly Desperate for a Break in the Monotony"
From *Trouping for the Troops: Fun-Making at the Front* (1919, pp. 140–43).

In the next town we arrived late, having been sent by motor and lost our way—not so late however as we should have been by train for the tracks were now so congested by "blessé" trains relaying the wounded to hospitals further down the line that all train schedules had been practically abandoned. We were hustled into another car with very little supper and were again driven miles through the cold to the outskirts of the town where we played to an audience of twenty-five hundred men who had been in quarantine for "ages" as they said and who were feeling perfectly desperate for a break in the monotony.

One of the "Y"[MCA] women and a Red Cross nurse came back to the dressing room of the hut to tell me confidentially that the men had worked until seven that night decorating a new hall that they themselves had renovated and painted and that they had been scheming for days to "get up" a supper after the show and would be heart broken unless we came. We all looked at each other in despair for, in spite of having had better living accommodations in the S.O.S. [Services of Supply] than on any other part of the tour, the depressed state of the men to whom we played, or the great number of hospital shows, or the constant rain or something or other had pulled us down in a few days more than all the real hardships at the front—and we were so tired, as one of the girls put it—that our very souls ached. The men of our unit tried to explain this for us but the inevitable answer came back—"Just come for a few minutes. They haven't seen any girls for so long. It will do them so much good." We knew the speech by heart and we had often responded to it when we were longing and aching for our beds, and to-night on the way out we had pledged ourselves to each other not to give in to it again, and now we were all ashamed to refuse them and also ashamed to go back on our word to ourselves and to each other.

I looked at the weaker of the two girls and said: "Well, how about it?" She answered that she would do whatever the rest of us did.

The men of our unit argued, and truthfully, that it was the girls that the boys wanted to see and that they would never be missed and were going home.

When we saw how hard the boys must have worked to decorate the barracks and with what pleasure they watched each course of the supper come onto the long tables we were glad that we had not disappointed them but, Ye gods, there were hundreds of them and they had a band waiting to play dance music and there were only three of us.

I shall never forget that dance—it seemed to me I'd only been turned in one direction when some one from out [sic] the long lines of uniforms that penned us in would seize me and turn me around in another direction and some one else would snatch me from him and step on me, and then release me to another before he'd even consoled me and so on and so on for hours and here and there out of the corner of my eye I could catch fleeting glimpses of a pink dress and a tan coloured dress and I knew the same thing was happening to the other two girls.

Some time later on we leaned back in the car too exhausted to speak. When we were about half way home one of the girls said wearily—"Well, I've only *one* life to give for my country, thank God!"

And the next morning I thought my time had come to give mine. The expected had happened—after dancing with men just recovering from Flu and just taking it on—I'd got one of the "going or coming" germs and it was only by the aid of all my will power, [vaudeville performers] Mr. [Will] Morrisey's rum, and Miss [Elizabeth] Brice's quinine, that I was able to keep going until we had played our last performance in the S. O. S.—temperature 104—and fallen exhausted into the first train that would get us back to Paris.

The power of the doughnut: Salvation Army poster by James Allen St. John, ca. 1918.
Library of Congress, Prints and Photographs Division, reproduction no. LC-USZC4-3172.

Helen Purviance was born in Huntington, IN. Purviance and Chicago's Margaret Sheldon are credited with creating the first doughnuts for the AEF during their 1917–18 service in France as Salvation Army volunteers. Working close to the front lines, they were often in danger. The doughnut became a powerful symbol to doughboys far from home and of Salvation Army services to them. A 14 May 1936 *New York Times* article stated that Purviance had distributed some 1 million doughnuts during the war, but they became a painful reminder to her of "the horrors of war." She eventually rose to the rank of lieutenant colonel in the Salvation Army.

Elizabeth Foxwell

"Fortunately for me it was a dud."
From "A Doughgirl on the Firing Line"
The Forum Dec. 1918: 648–56

When a French soldier is wounded, and knows he is "going West," he asks for his wife, an Englishman calls for his sweetheart, but an American wants his mother. And the thought of that mother is carried with him like an indelible print from the training camps in America, across three thousand miles of water, and remains with him when he goes "over the top" and into that unknown country from which many never return.

I don't believe there are any big mothers in America, I mean big in stature, for every soldier speaks of her as "little mother."

"Say, when I get home—" Well you just ought to hear some of the things these boys of ours tell me they are going to do when they get home. Some are going to sleep two weeks but most of them are going to eat. So I just want to warn you, you American mothers, stock the pantry right up to its top-most shelf with all the things he likes best because he has already decided what he wants for that first dinner at home.

Our organization sent women workers to France that your boys may not miss you quite so much. We try to create a little of the home atmosphere and with a woman's hands help them over the rough spots of homesickness, wounds, or any of the other hurts that come to the fighting man. Our huts do not always look like a home. Sometimes it's a real, honest-to-goodness hut that can be taken to pieces and put together again at a moment's notice. Another time it may be a tent, or a corner in some shell-torn house.

The boys very rarely call us sister but very, very often you hear a twenty-seven year old girl addressed as "mother." If it wasn't for the beautiful tribute in that word, "mother," one would have to smile when it's used by a man old enough to be her father.

After I had been in Paris a few days, I went down to a camp of thirty-five thousand soldiers, where the Salvation Army has six huts, to learn something of housekeeping in a strange country under difficulties. The boys seemed glad to see American girls and many of them came over and bashfully shook hands with us. Some of them hadn't seen any girls from the States for months.

Where the First Doughnuts Were Fried

From there our Col. [William S.] Barker, of the S. A., took three other girls and myself out in the car to look for some troops who needed mothering. Our destination proved to be a big camp of the First Ammunition Train, which supplies ammunition to the First Division, America's famous shock troops. The boys absolutely refused to let us go, so Col. Barker left us with them. It was at this camp and on this division that the first American doughnut was given its try-out.

"What can we make to eat out of the things we have that will be American and taste good to the boys?" said one of the girls.

"A doughnut," promptly replied Margaret Sheldon, of Chicago, Ill., and a doughnut it was. We had no rolling pin, so the dough had to be patted into shape, and then came the question of how to cut it out. That problem was solved with the top of a baking-powder can and the hole, for whoever heard of a doughnut without a hole, was made with a camphor ice tube. I fried the first doughnut and saw it eaten by an American soldier. One of the boys remarked a short time after that as he was munching one of our doughnuts, "if this is war, let it continue."

When orders came for the men to move to the front, the Commanding Officer did not think we would be allowed to go, but just the same he supplied each of us with a helmet, two gas masks, and a shelter-half. (A shelter-half is part of a tent and the other half is carried by the fellow who shares the tent with you.)

Under Boche Guns

It was decided that we were to go to the front after all. On our arrival in the Toul Sector, the boys made dugouts for us, we opened our canteen, and everything was decidedly comfy considering we were in range of the enemy's guns. One of the boys gave me a dog, a French shepherd dog, whom we called "Sancey," and whenever the Boche planes began to bomb us that dog ran immediately to the dugout where she knew she would be fairly safe. But I can't say that the doughboys or doughgirls displayed quite so much common sense. Most of us ran out to see the planes, and on one occasion one of them flew so close to the ground that we could see the aviator. Several of the boys, and a couple of the girls, too, got rifles and shot at him. Of course this was very dangerous and strictly against regulations, for it only proved to the Boche, what he already suspected, that troops were billeted there.

It was at this time that the General in command of that division asked that all American women doing war work in France assist at the hospitals during a drive. I volunteered and was sent to a field hospital for gas and shell-shock men. I worked in the evacuation ward trying to make the men as comfortable as possible while awaiting their turn. We washed the blood from their faces, took away their handkerchiefs which were soaked with the gas, and gave them fresh pieces of gauze. For some we wrote letters, and if we had time washed their hands. We always made hot chocolate, soups, or cooling drinks for them. A doctor said to me, "If you women didn't do anything but walk through the wards so the boys could see you, and hear you talk, it would help." Another doctor told us that the hospital attendants were more gentle with their patients because women were there.

The Sleepers in the Poppy Fields

One afternoon I was feeling a bit "fed-up" with remaining indoors, so I left one girl in charge of the hut and suggested to the others that we take a walk. We felt that it was selfish to be merely taking a pleasure stroll, and decided to go up the hill and decorate the three American graves there. They were by a poppy field, and gathering great armfuls of these brilliant blooms, we made the resting place of those American boys a mass of pink and crimson flowers.

"Let's go down the other side of the hill to the hospital and leave the rest there," I said. "We have so many left." So we did and I hope they cheered up the sick boys.

Whenever we find an American grave (they are all marked), we take pictures of it, and if possible get the address of the relatives and write them, telling its location. It must be some comfort to those at home to know that *his* grave is being cared for by another American woman. The French people incidentally are very kind in this respect, and often the kiddies carry bouquets of flowers to put on freshly made graves of "Les Americains."

The Lure of the Kitchen

Somebody once asked me how many batches of doughnuts we make in a day. I couldn't say, because we make one right after the other, as fast as we can. As soon as the boys find out we are making doughnuts they begin to line up, and as fast as they are cooked, they take them out of the pot with a twig.

Most of the work done by the ammunition boys must, of a necessity, be done at night, so I kept my hut open all night.

An officer said to me, "Adjutant Purviance, since your hut has been open at night I find my men have fewer accidents and less repairing to do. They don't want to miss that piece of pie and cup of hot chocolate."

We hadn't had any mail for almost a month and the boys were "pretty low," as they expressed it. They hung around the kitchen more than ever. Some of them scraped pans and washed mugs because they wanted a chance to talk to us. It was very hard to get flour at that time, the transportation facilities being especially bad, and one day one of the boys came in the kitchen and said, "I know why you can't get any flour." Of course we all asked, "Why?"

"Because," he said with a grin, "they are making so many doughboys now."

While I was running two huts about a kilometer and a half apart, I started out for the other one late one evening. About halfway there I met the girl I had left in charge marching along at the head of a whole company of soldiers. In answer to my question she replied, "the Captain said we could entertain these boys for the evening." So back to the hut we went and I gave the top sergeants fifteen minutes to select the best talent in the lot. They sang, gave recitations, danced and told funny stories. They all like to sing, also to play games; blind man's bluff, drop the handkerchief, and romping games that go back to the days of their childhood parties.

The Fight on the Soissons Front

We arrived at the Soissons front about nine o'clock one night and the billeting officer assigned us to quarters for the night. We always carry blankets, cots, and sometimes mattresses. When we got to the house assigned to us, or rather what was left of the house, we found it already occupied, so back we went. We didn't want to look for another place because we knew all the corners would be harboring sleeping soldiers. So we just sat and waited for our friend the billeting officer. He didn't get back until 4 o'clock, so we decided to sleep some other time and began to make out doughnuts, pies, and hot chocolate for the coming day. Everyone had left the village but two old ladies, who had positively refused to go, and they still pottered around in their garden perfectly indifferent to the shells the Boche sent over at frequent intervals.

The next night we made our beds in an ammunition truck. You have never seen anything so beautifully kept as the engines in those trucks and the boys are justly proud of them. During the Cantigny drive our General sent a message to the front asking if the line was still holding and the answer came back, "it will hold as long as you continue to keep us supplied with ammunition."

Our boys are such splendid fighters! When they start after the Hun nothing stops them, not even their own barrage. Many of them have been wounded simply because they wouldn't stop, and went right through our own artillery fire, but as the boys all say they want to "see those Germans pushing up the daisies."

I heard a captured German General say, "your men are wonderful fighters. You have organized and trained an army in a few months that would have taken us five years."

Our boys told me they had captured machine gun nests where German women had been strapped to the guns just as the men were. In fact not far from us there was a woman among the prisoners.

Putting women in the trenches, and sawdust in their bread, were some of the other things Germany had to resort to before the end. I happened to find some of their bread and saw the sawdust but I wanted to be sure, so one of the doctors examined it too. A German prisoner stood and watched us, then said, "the Kaiser baked that bread."

. . . . One of the hardest things I ever had to do was to tell a boy of his mother's death. His captain came to me with two letters, one written to him by the boy's sister and the other for the boy.

"Look here, you're a woman and can do this better than I can," he said, putting the two letters in my hand. Then he sent the boy to me. He was just a youngster, only seventeen years old. When I finished talking with him, he said, "I guess my sister thinks I don't care what happens now, but she's wrong. I'm going to live a clean, straight life so I'll be able to meet my mother when it's all over."

For the Days of Waiting

I have a message to you mothers, wives, sisters, and sweethearts of America, a message from your boys in khaki. I am trying to tell you what it means to those boys to have some of their womenkind with them in France, and how much more it's going to mean to them now that the fighting has stopped. Those fighters of ours whom we affectionately call "our boys," but whom the Germans speak of as "men," will need us much more now. America can't send too many of her best men and women to help the man in khaki through that tiresome period of waiting to come home.

I have been in the Salvation Army for ten years, serving mankind. I have been within sound of the guns for fifteen months, and twice, during the whole time, I was, I must admit, what is so expressively called "scared to death." A bomb did it once and a shell the other time. When the bomb fell I was out in the vegetable garden with some other girls and several soldiers. Somebody yelled and automatically everybody threw themselves flat on the ground. The bomb hit near us and made a hole large enough to put a small size house in. The other time I was standing in the little curtained off part of the tent we used for our sleeping quarters, when I heard the swish of a shell. I knew it wasn't from our guns because there was no report. So I faced about with the vague idea of dodging it. It landed all right but fortunately for me it was a dud and didn't explode, or I wouldn't be here now.

When we got ready to move to the Verdun front, the Colonel said no women could go.

"Oh, Colonel, you don't mean that," said one of our girls. "You can't expect us to stay here when our boys are going?"

"You can't go," he repeated, "you will be killed."

"Please don't say we can't go, Colonel. We can't leave our boys but we can die with them."

Eighty percent of the S. A. workers in France are women, and I am glad I was permitted to be one of the first four that went to the front. I have been on six different battle fronts. When I first went to Toul I saw Mont Sec and was there again in time to see it captured. . . .

Esther Sayles Root (Adams) (1894–1981)

Marjorie Crocker, left, and Esther Sayles Root. From Over Periscope
Pond *(1918), frontispiece.*

Daughter of publisher Charles Towner Root and granddaughter of
Civil War composer George F. Root, Esther Sayles Root (nicknamed
"Rootie") graduated from Smith College in 1915. Her letters in *Over
Periscope Pond* (coauthored with Marjorie Crocker [Fairbanks], 1918)
relate her experiences in Paris assisting refugees for the organization
Students Atelier Reunions, which was led by Ernest Warburton
Shurtleff, a Congregational minister, and his wife, Helen.

She later served as drama critic for the *Morning Telegraph.* Root
married Franklin Pierce Adams (aka "F.P.A." in the *New Yorker*) in
May 1925 and had four children. A member of Alice Paul's National
Woman's Party, she achieved success in having a passport issued
with her maiden name (something prohibited by the State Department at the time); the passport was listed as "Esther Sayles Root,
wife of Franklin Pierce Adams."

"Piles, piles, piles of stone"

From *Over Periscope Pond* (1918): 29–36, 236–56

Paris
November 26, 1916
Dearest Mother:

. . . . We have found that people can get a furnished room for thirty centimes a day and up. Awful little rooms, dens of darkness and disease, can be found (only occasionally, praise be) for three francs a week; but I can't consider those. I saw one yesterday—a mother and two little girls live there, and it was about the size of the cabin in our motor-boat, but made the latter seem vast and airy by comparison. With the prices of food and coal high, and constantly soaring, the poor people can just make out their rent and food, but cannot buy clothes. Shoes are thirty francs and up. You can figure it out for yourself. With our help, however, many, many poor families can get along that would otherwise be destitute. Sometimes we can give a girl a suit which will enable her to present herself for a far better position than she could hope to obtain in rags. Sometimes boys can go to school if they have warm new shoes, a black apron, and an overcoat, when without them they would stay at home and shiver in idleness. Warm strong clothing not only gives a new lease to health, but to life as a whole. You should see the little girls when I give them a hair-ribbon or a dress for their doll, if they have one.

.... In some cases we go so far as to move families from crowded, dirty, unsavory quarters to as clean and as airy a place as we can find in proportion to their income. We then guarantee their rent for three months and help them to furnish. . . .

The field work is the visiting and investigation of applicants. The war work of the Students Atelier Reunions has become known by word of mouth among the refugees. Of course, the reports and results of our work travel like wildfire and we are inundated with requests. After receiving a letter from a refugee the case is looked up by two field workers and reported at a meeting of the committee the following Saturday morning. A vote is taken as to what to do and how much to give if it is decided to give anything. The people are then told to present themselves at the Vestiaire and we give them what they need. Every type of man, woman, and child has crossed our threshold even within my month of service. How I love them all!

. . . . The next big branch of work is fitting out the blind. There is more pathos, gayety, and inspiration on Tuesday and Friday afternoons than in all the rest of the week. After the men are wounded at the front they are brought back through a chain of relief stations, "postes de secours," to hospitals, and finally to a Paris hospital. The blind are allowed to recuperate here at the Val de Grace or the Quinze-Vingt (big hospitals) and are then sent away, usually to the country to learn a trade or to rejoin their families, or both. They must give up their military clothes, underclothes, and shoes when they are discharged, and are given only the poorest kind of civilian clothes in exchange. This is where we step in to give them decent clothes. In many cases they are not given civilian clothes at all, although I don't understand the Government system enough to see how that is possible. So Miss Hodges, our representative in work for the blind, brings five or six of the most needy and touching cases to us and we fit them out.

. . . Such brave fellows! It is an exception to see one downcast or morose, but when you do, your heart aches twice as much, not only for them, but for the many gay ones who have conquered despair. One boy twenty-four years old was wounded in the leg and dragged himself along the ground half conscious, to find he was dragging himself toward the German trenches. At this point he was struck again and his eyes put out. He lay between the trenches under fire for days, unconscious most of the time and feigning death the rest. By a miracle he escaped being killed. He was picked up and taken to a hospital; has been there six months, and is now starting out to learn a trade—in the dark. I love to do what I can for them, especially as this is my one chance to know the French poilu.

. . . .The blind soldiers are always interested to know what their new clothes look like. "C'est de quel couleur, Mademoiselle?" "Dark brown," I say, "and I will give you a brown and white tie." "Ah que je serai chic, moi!" One of his comrades would nudge him and say, "Je voudrais bien avoid les jeux pour the voir, maintenant, mon vieux! C'est vrai que tu vais the marier?" (I would like to have eyes to see you now, old fellow; is it true you are just going to be married?)

Then they laugh and thank me "mille fois" and shake hands and wish me good luck. Sometimes I walk down the street with them and guide them along. I admire their medals and tell them that the passers-by are looking at them, etc. We never say the word "aveugle" (blind), but "blessé" (wounded).

September 9, 1917
Dearest Father:
. . . How many pictures I've seen marked, "Somewhere in France," or, "Results of German Shells." How endlessly have I pored over Sunday supplements or watched miles of film click by, trying always to imagine myself really standing on French soil, seeing real things. But the pictures were always just black and white, and I never managed to step into them.

The refugees at the Vestiaire tell vivid stories, and they all have that inborn dramatic instinct which can make live the scenes they describe. But even from their background I had no idea of the look and atmosphere of the ruined towns as they now are. No one ever told me that the trenches taken from the Germans a few months ago would now be half hidden by long grass and brilliant red poppies, nor that summer sunshine could ever soften the grimness of barbed wire and dug-outs. Yesterday I saw for myself.

Compiègne is the sentinel to the "zone des armées." At the railroad station you must present your sauf-conduit before you go through the gate, and frown as you do so, for certainly the official will frown at you. The streets are full of soldiers and officers, blue with them, and great military trucks grind past at every turn. Even the churchyard is filled with lines of military wagons, and horses were tethered at its portals.

.... Our military cars, painted dull gray with the numbers in white across the wind shield, were waiting to take us on our wonderful journey. As we left the narrow streets of Compiègne, we passed several motors bearing important-looking officers going to or from the front; they tore around corners in just my idea of a warlike way—very little gold braid, but business-like and grim.

The country was lovely: rolling fields, and deep woods, rich with foliage. My idea of a devastated region had been a large plain, covered with small ruined villages, blackened by smoke. I had pictured everything bare and muddy—no grass, lowering clouds; but here was blazing sunlight, and such grass and flowers as I had never seen.

At Noyon we were joined by a French lieutenant, who acted as guide to us, and was High Mogul to all guards and officials along our route. He looked skeptical of a party of women, even Americans (who are known to be wild), tearing along on the roads where only soldiers, trucks, and beasts of burden are seen.

The crops interested me very much. Large fields of wheat and barley, as well as trim lines of lettuce and garden truck, were on each side of the road near every settlement. I asked who planted them. "Different people," said our lieutenant; "the people who have been living here right along under the Germans, the soldiers who delivered the territory last March, the civil population who came back to their homes when the Boches were driven out."

Until March 18th, the Germans held French territory up to the line passing through Rossières, Andréhy, Lassigny, Ribecourt, and Soissons. They retreated on that date, and the present line passes just west of Saint-Quentin, La Fère, and Barésis. Our route was a big circle through the section between these lines among the towns most lately relinquished by the invader.

I felt reluctant to be whisked along so fast, for I wanted to see just how these bridges had been blown up. I wanted to ask that old man over there, hoeing in the field with a tiny little girl beside him in a black apron, what he had seen and felt, and how he liked the Boches. But we seemed always to keep the same pace.

At Chauny we slowed up, however. We passed down an aisle of ruins, and stopped in a big square. We were told: "They are shelling the town, so that you run a risk if you stop here, but they seem to be lazy to-day, so don't worry." I was so glad to get out of the car and wander around according to my fancy, that I didn't give a thought to the possibility of shells. And I couldn't see why they should want to keep on firing, as there didn't seem more to do to the place. I stood at first and looked about me. Not one roof to be seen—just walls, and not more than one or two stories of these. Nothing horizontal—just the perpendicular skeletons of buildings, and piles, piles, piles of stone in between.

The streets have been cleared of rubbish, by the French, so that the square or "place" looked as neat and ready for market-day as though the market-women might come at any moment with their pushcarts, station themselves in the center, and display piles of carrots, cherries, potatoes, and radishes to tempt the passing throng.

But the passing throng had passed somewhere else. We saw nobody. On one side was a wall marked "Théâtre"—just the front of it left, all the rest ruins. Across the square was a large building with "Palais de Justice" carved over the portal, portions of the front ripped away so that we could see the different rooms and central staircase leading up, and up, to nothing.

Down the cobbled streets which radiated from the square were the remains of the shops and homes of the people of Chauny. Ruins everywhere. The houses had evidently been blown up from within, causing the roofs and floors to fall in a heap into the cellar, so that it was difficult to walk in and look about. The town has, of course, been shelled as well as mined; the Germans were determined to wipe it out completely, so that the iron and sugar industries which made Chauny well known may never be resumed.

The strangest kind of things would be lying in the piles of débris—an iron bedstead, twisted and red with rust, an old baby carriage, a boot, a candlestick, all sorts of little domestic things. In many houses the tiled fireplaces were intact, and stood up among all the wreckage. Our lieutenant climbed into one of the houses and brought back a few tiles which he gave us. Mine is a heavenly turquoise blue, smooth and perfect. It is the one relic that I cared to keep. I prefer it to a charred brick or a bent piece of iron. It was there in its place in the war, during the burning and pillaging, and weathered the bombs and the shells.

Through the back windows were vistas of grass and trees. I saw an enchanting ravine with a stony brook running through it, and gardens, full of rank grass and weeds. Here and there a holly bush looked about in surprise at being so neglected this year.

The church in Chauny is only half destroyed. Most of the roof has been blown up, and the west end of the nave is piled high with wreckage, but the altar is untouched and there is enough roof left to shelter about ten rows of seats. A rough partition of wood and tarred paper has been built across the middle of the church, which divides the piles of broken stone, open to the blazing sunlight, from the altar half hidden and dim.

It was very quiet. I heard a bird chirping near by, and saw two sparrows fly through an opening and perch on a cornice over the cross. There is not much left in Chauny even for a bird.

The road leading north runs beside an embankment high enough to screen a motor from view. Where this embankment stops, a huge screen has been built of boughs woven in and out of a wire foundation; thus the road is hidden for miles, and military trucks, ammunition trains, themselves "camouflés," pass to and fro unobserved.

Near Villquiers-Aumont we began to see the cut-down fruit trees....what we saw were rolling green fields, with fruit trees lying prone in even rows, their naked branches—"Bare, ruined choirs where late the sweet birds sang"—ruined carefully and deliberately.

We stopped near an abrupt little hill. It looked like a giant thimble, with a rustic summer-house on top. This was once [the kaiser's son] Prince Eitel Friedrich's lookout, and as we climbed up the carefully made stone steps, we saw more and more of the wonderful view he had chosen. French landscapes stretched away on every side, smooth fields, winding roads, and poplars. The group of poilus who were stationed in the look-out gave us a gay welcome. They were ready with information about the surrounding countryside, and pointed out the various villages in the distance. The officer in charge lent us his field-glasses and showed us to the north the spires of the cathedral at Saint-Quentin—still held by the Boches.

We took a détour in order to see the grave of Sergeant [James Rogers] McConnell, the American aviator who was killed last spring. A French flag and two American flags nailed to a wooden cross mark the grave; fifty yards away are a few splinters of iron and wood, the remains of his airplane, which indicate the spot where he fell. Some splinters of wood, some rusty bits of iron, part of the engine, are all that is left of his aeroplane. As I looked back towards the grave I saw our soldier chauffeur stooping to place a bunch of wild poppies below the flags. He walked back to his place at the wheel without knowing that I had seen him. It was a small thing, but I felt grateful to the American who had made a simple Frenchman wish to pay this tribute. I felt, too, a warm pride to think of this corner of a foreign field (to paraphrase Rupert Brooke) that is forever America!

We went next to Flavy-le-Martel. This town is half ruined and is inhabited only by soldiers. The great sight is a ruined factory, which is now a grotesque pile of rubbish—wheels and boilers and chimneys; the mass of broken stone and twisted iron is heaped to an immense height and in extent it looked to one like an acre of pure destruction.

Suddenly we heard discomforting sounds—guns, big guns, and not very far away. The entrance gate to the factory had been locked and barred with a sign, "No Admittance," in large letters, and we had to enter through a hole in the fence, but certainly that couldn't mean that we were doing anything *dangerous?* One of the soldiers working near by motioned upwards, and we caught sight of a Boche aeroplane disappearing in a big white cloud—lesser white clouds kept multiplying as the French anti-aircraft guns fired on. Each shot sounded like hitting a barn door with a baseball—only fifty times as loud. I was all for standing with my neck craned waiting to see what would happen next, but the soldiers gave one laconic look (if a look can be laconic) at the signs in the heavens, and walked off to the "abri" or shelter. Our lieutenant asked us to follow, so down we plunged into a little cellar-like place after the soldiers.

"Five men were wounded here yesterday by pieces of flying shell," said one of them; "so, Mon Dieu! it is not worth the trouble to make one's self a target to-day."

That seemed sensible enough, but it had never occurred to me that anything would ever come down and hit *me.* I'm not a soldier, I'm not even French, and everything about the front has always been a name to me until now. What am I usually doing the first week of July? I'm helping the kids set off firecrackers down on the beach—on a good old American beach; or getting the mail at the post-office to read the latest war news. *Zum-zum!* and here I am crouched down in an abri with some poilus, and a German biplane a mile in the air straight over my head. Wouldn't it be funny if—I wonder how thick the roof of this place is, anyway? *Zum, zum,* ZUM! How foolish to drop bombs on a place that is destroyed, anyway.

The firing became less frequent and the explosions farther off. We climbed out to the great outdoors again, and looked around. Nothing to be seen or heard. Just as we started off, a last *zum!* and a fleeting glimpse of the Boche disappeared gayly into a cloud. That was a week ago; I'm wondering if they have got him by now.

Along the road on the way to Ham were rows of neat little brick and stone houses, so unlike anything I had seen that their very neatness looked strange. "The soldiers have already begun rebuilding," said the lieutenant. And they have done well, may I add; the architecture is of an unimaginative, cubelike variety, but a touch of poetry is supplied by the white muslin curtains and climbing nasturtiums! The soldiers, working with sleeves rolled up and with gorgeous red sashes round their waists, smiled and waved as we passed, and if we had slowed down who knows but that we should have had an invitation to tea; with a Boche avion only just lost from view.

It was an interesting road all the way. We met a priest trotting comfortably down the road on a fat chestnut mare. His gown fluttered and his beads swung by his side in time to the horse's gait. We all felt included in his smile as he lifted his shallow-crowned, wide-brimmed hat in greeting; we Americans bowed, the militaires saluted inflexibly.

. . . . Beyond Roye about eight kilometers "as the shell flies," the old first-line German trenches can be seen from the road. Barbed-wire entanglements stretch away to left and right, half hidden in the grass, and dug-outs covered by heavy logs occur at intervals. Where the trenches began to run along close to the road, we left the motors and climbed down among the narrow, rustic walks that are trenches. The floors and walls are made of small boughs nailed nearly one inch apart, and the depth of the trenches is a little over six feet. They turn and twist unbelievably—apparently following the track of a spotted snake with a tummy-ache; and communication trenches, "boyaux," fork off every fifty feet or so, making a network of passages.

I saw a tube of iron with a star-shaped end which interested me; the lieutenant hastily called out that it was a hand grenade. I had read too many war stories to be inclined to have anything more to do with it, so I passed obediently by; the next minute I caught my foot in some infernal machine and my heart leaped as I wildly clutched at the sides of trench for support. It was a twisted bedspring.

Near by was an opening twenty-five feet square with dug-outs along the edge, where officers evidently lived. There was a rustic table under a lattice-trimmed shelter, and a flight of birch steps led to the sleeping quarters!

The lavish grass and flowers constantly impressed me. Around the trenches up to the very edges of the shell holes, over the famous strip called "No Man's Land," grows to-day a gorgeous carpet of green grass and wild flowers. I like to think that Nature has already begun to heal the scars of war.

. . . . [J]ust as I did not at first distinguish the signs of war, so I did not fully consider until afterward the completeness of the destruction we had seen. In the section of forty miles square that we skirted, not one bridge is left—the only ones now in existence are of temporary military construction. The same is true of telephone and telegraph poles—not one remains. Also there is not a stick of furniture of any sort except what was too heavy to be taken away, such as pulpits and big tables, which were hacked to pieces and are of no value now. That the furniture was not blown up with the houses I am sure, for not a piece can be found in the ruins, and I looked carefully for any trace. Germany must be full of French furniture, and what it is all wanted for I can't imagine.

It is wonderful what vistas can be thrown open by the experiences of one day. I never again can hear of any one who comes from Chauny or Roye or Lassigny without seeing row upon row of deserted, ruined houses. I never can hear of a fortune lost in the war without picturing the ruined sugar factory at Flavy-le-Martel. And yet the sight of men and mules and engines clearing out the canal at Ham is more significant than either of these, for it means that the energy which once built the cities of France is deathless. A new beginning is being made within sound of the guns; and we are helping. *We are helping!!*

Grace Gallatin Thompson Seton (1872–1952)

Grace Gallatin Thompson Seton, n.d. Library of Congress, Prints and Photographs Division, reproduction no. LC-DIG-ggbain-06053.

Born in Sacramento, Grace Gallatin became a noted travel writer, lecturer, and suffragist. In 1896, she married Ernest Thompson Seton, an author of nature and boys' books; their daughter became the bestselling novelist Anya Seton. They divorced in 1935.

From 1917 to 1919, Seton spearheaded the Woman's Motor Unit of Le Bien Etre du Blesse, a unit supported by the New York Women's City Club that transported food to diet kitchens at aid stations in France. She was in France from June to October 1918 to manage this unit, and she was decorated by the French government for her service. After the war she traveled in Europe to see reconstruction efforts; participated in the effort to ratify the 19th amendment to the

Constitution; and explored Latin America, China, Egypt, India, Vietnam, and the Philippines.

"I Simply Disappeared through a Hole in the Floor"
From "Tapering Off the War"
Goodwin's Weekly 14 Dec. 1918: 6–7

. . . . At one kitchen where [Red Bank, NJ's] Estelle Greenawalt was stationed . . . the days of monotonously doing errands for the welfare of the wounded were varied by days and weeks of thrills. . . . The German advance in June and early July caught this hospital so that it was evacuated three times in as many weeks. Think of what that means with personnel and equipment for 1,500 beds, and the wounded as well!—and then came the awful days of the middle of July, before and during the great push, when the Germans were within a few miles of Paris and hospitals were bombed and raided and shelled.

Estelle's ambulance [unit] of 1,500 beds passed through 5,000 wounded Frenchmen and a sprinkling of Americans in twenty-four hours, when three operating theaters were going each night and day and nobody, surgeons or nurses, slept more than two hours out of the twenty-four, and Estelle was sent down to Paris in Mrs. [Louise Hartshorn] Leeds' car, nearly a hundred miles away, to get supplies which could brook no delay—anti-tetanus serum, anti-gangrene serum and cases of Red Cross bandages.

And a few days later another trip, without stopping for rest, on the neglected war-torn roads of France, she again dashed to Paris to get armitures, back-rests, linen and cigarettes and chocolate, and between times she helped the nurses. . . . [I]n September she was the first woman to cross the Vesle river in the victorious advance of the allies.

Another girl was stationed with the Edith Cavell truck in a hospital near Chalon-sur-Marne, and daily the bombardment continued getting closer and closer until the order to evacuate was given, after a shell had damaged several of the barraques. . . . Every one stuck to her post until the last moment. . . .Two of the nurses were injured by flying shrapnel.

. . . . I have been in air raids in London and Paris . . . and, of course under shell fire in my inspection tours.

At one French camp I was the guest of the colonel for several days. He took me much nearer things than he should have, I'm afraid. In fact, we were between the guns and the village which was being shelled, safe, because the shells were flying over our heads.

You know I became so used to shells, bombs and shrapnel that I could distinguish their size and kind by the noise they made coming through the air.

On July 20, just two days after the big push, I visited a base hospital in the Chateau-Thierry section. It was a 1,200-bed hospital in a half-wood, half-tents horse barracks. Twice the hospital had been pushed back in a German advance.

The nurses and surgeons had arranged two hours of sleep out of twenty-four for five days. I arrived late in the afternoon, and in spite of their fatigue they insisted on preparing tea for me. Just because I was Anglo-Saxon they thought I could not get along without it.

There was one American nurse at the hospital. She came in to meet me. That one woman had charge of the hopeless ward, that one in which men were so badly wounded they could not live. She had no one but two orderlies to help her, and the orderlies of France are not like ours. They do no nursing and know nothing about it.

However, about two and a half miles away there was an American aviation camp. Every night when he was released from duty, one of the young American aviators would walk over to the hospital to do what he could to help his country-woman. He would arrive about 10 o'clock and leave at 3, night after night.

That spirit has impressed me as one of the sweetest and most splendid I encountered in all my experiences.

The wounded were still coming in from the big drive, and so many men needed attention that I myself volunteered to help this nurse and her gallant champion that night.

The nurses' room was simply a little 6 by 8 corner, partitioned off from the wards with horse blankets. In there I slipped on my Red Cross apron and veil.

We were allowed no lights. One feeble little lantern hung in that hopelessly wounded ward. The floor was simply dirt and the place smelt like a stable.

I helped the nurse give one poor blesse a hypodermic, and right in the middle of it I happened to step backward and—well, I simply disappeared through a hole in the floor. That shows what a condition it was in. I hit my head on the next cot and that broke the fall.

Well, the nurse was using her last hypodermic needle, and if that one had broken I don't know what she would have done, the men were suffering so. While she was at work I collected all the old, rusty, bent needles I could find and took them out to sterilize them and tune them up as best I could in case of emergency.

I was busy with this work when suddenly there was the most terrific explosion. A Boche plane had spotted the hospital and bombed it. The bomb fell in the neighboring field. Of course all the men began to moan. It was ghastly. We could hear the motor overhead.

"How soon does the next one land?" I asked the nurse, and she replied, "In about three minutes." But before that time was up I heard a whirr and buzzing and the American aviators in the neighboring camp were driving the Boche away.

Those are the conditions under which our motor drivers have worked all the time. That is over now. But they are needed, and needed badly, in reconstruction work for the next six months.

Everyone realizes that it is impossible to stop this war work suddenly. It has to be tapered. . . . I want the Woman's Motor Unit of Le Bien Etre du Blesse to taper its work to a splendid close and be worthy [of] the continued admiration of the French people.

Josephine Sherzer (1892–1964)

Born in Ypsilanti, Josephine Sherzer was the daughter of William H. Sherzer, professor of geology at Eastern Michigan University, and Maude Jerome, a cousin of Winston Churchill. She graduated from the University of Michigan in 1915 and was a Red Cross searcher in France during World War I. She later served as president of the Association of Visiting Teachers of the Michigan Board of Education.

In this account she describes the duties involved in her Red Cross work.

"Yearning for Some Information"
Letter (n.d.)
Published in *The Michigan Alumnus* Jan.1919: 251–52

I told you in my last letter that I had to be transferred from refugee work, did I not? They told me at headquarters to-day that it is permissible to give you a fairly detailed account of what my work will be. My official title will be "Searcher," and I shall be attached to some hospital, where I shall have an office which is supposed to be made as comfortable and home-like as possible.

Every week I must send to the Paris Bureau reports on the men seriously wounded or too sick to write home themselves. Every morning I shall receive a list of names of men about whom inquiries are made by friends. I must find out whether any of these men are in our hospital, and, if so, send a report on their condition and whereabouts. I must keep all these names filed in a card catalogue, for future reference in case the men might come through our hospital at some later date.

Whenever a man dies it is my duty to write a letter to his next of kin. Such letters must be sympathetic and contain the fullest details, giving the date of death, an account of his sickness, and any personal message; also the details of the funeral, a description of the grave, and a flower from one of the wreaths which the Mother may keep.

The Paris Bureau publishes on the first of every month a book containing a list of the men reported missing, and a supplement on the fifteenth of the month. This contains a list of the men whose fate is unknown, and whose families are yearning for some information. Since the missing man's companions may know something about him, it is an important duty of the Searcher to interview any man of the company who may pass through that hospital. If desired, the Searcher may write letters at the direct dictation of the sick or wounded.

If the Searcher finds in the hospital a man who is concerned about the welfare of his family at home, it is her duty to get the name and address of the family, to obtain accurately the nature of his worry and to write a full history of his case to the "Home Service" section, Paris. The man can be given assurance that the welfare of his family will be immediately investigated, and upon receipt of a cable in Washington, some representative will call on his family in his home town and give them whatever aid they need.

If men in the hospital are not receiving their mail, it is the business of the Searcher to attend to this. If the family at home are not receiving their allotment, the Searcher attends to it. If the soldier is not receiving his salary, it is the business of the Searcher to look into the matter.

If lucky, I may have a stenographer; if no stenographer, I may use the typewriter myself, but there is every chance that there will be no typewriter even, in which case the writing will all have to be done by hand. Under favorable circumstances one Searcher has only 1,000 men to look after, but if help is short, one may have to do the best she can with 5,000 or even 10,000.

This is the most personal and most vital branch of the Red Cross service over here, and everyone thinks we are very fortunate to get into it. When my friend and I reported to this department office, the chief said that we were two of the huskiest specimens she had seen yet; that she was going to assign us to one of the hardest places in all France; and that if we were able to handle the situation, we would be doing something that no one had been able to do thus far.

Harriet Bard (Woodcock) Squiers (1864–1935)

Harriet Bard Squiers, n.d. Library of Congress, Prints and Photographs Division, reproduction no. LC-DIG-ggbain-27309.

Born in Sing Sing, NY, Harriet Bard Woodcock was a great-niece of multimillionaire John Jacob Astor; her father, William P. Woodcock Jr., was a physician. In November 1889, she became the second wife of Herbert Goldsmith Squiers, who served as U.S. first secretary in Peking during the Boxer Rebellion, minister to Panama, and envoy to Cuba. She and her husband converted to Catholicism, and she was stepmother to his four children and mother to three. Her husband died in 1911.

During World War I, she spearheaded the fundraising, building, and operating of a hospital (Hospice de St. Vincent de Paul) in Montmirail, France, and was awarded the Croix de Guerre after she and a skeleton staff cared for 600 wounded from the German offensive at Chateau-Thierry in June 1918. She also received a Médaille de la Reconaissance Française for her work with civilians. She later served in a French hospital in Strasburg and a U.S. hospital unit in Syria.

Squiers seems to have acquired a reputation for grace under duress. During the war she survived an accident in which she was pinned under a truck for more than an hour. Stated the "Editor's Note" to her diary excerpt published in the September 1920 *North American Review*, "She was shelled and bombed continually [during the war], but her experience in the Boxer Rebellion in Pekin[g], where she had to crawl about on her hands and knees to avoid being hit by the Boxer bullets which came in through the windows, had hardened her to that sort of thing" (319).

From "She Nursed Our Wounded at Chateau-Thierry"
New York Times 28 Jul 1918: 37

Hospice de St. Vincent de Paul
Montmirail, Marne, June 10, 1918
… Dearest Flora [her sister, Flora MacDonald Potter]:

This is the first day I have found to write to you of all we have passed through in the battle of Chateau-Thierry. As I wrote you, everyone was waiting breathlessly for the offensive, and when and where. I felt positively certain it would be here, for in history all Generals try to recover lost ground, and in this case especially, the Marne and Paris, which was the bitterest pill for the Germans.

As I wrote you, we had evacuated all our convalescents, and were painting our hospital and getting ready for the offensive.

Sunday night the General invited us to a dinner in the park of the chateau, and, oh, such a glorious night! Monday we invited them to dine here, also Captain Maurice, whom I knew at the siege of Peking, but—no dinner. For Maurice rushed in, saying the offensive had begun. The Huns had taken Chemin des Dames and were pouring down in streams, and that everyone was leaving Montmirail at once.

I immediately began to get the hospital ready, and by 5 on Tuesday we began to receive the wounded. One splendid surgeon was off on leave, but, thank God! another equally good arrived. Wednesday and Thursday I served at two operating tables from early morning till midnight. Bombs were bursting in the distance, and news came that the Huns were nearing Chateau-Thierry, only a few miles from us.

Everyone here worked like dogs.

* * *

Thursday night the medicine chief, the infirmiers, all left. They said they had orders to go. My maid fled with the rest.

I was left alone with Hoytie Wiborg [Mary Hoyt Wiborg, sister of expatriate American Sara Murphy], Lady Abinger, my English friend [possibly Lila Lucy Catherine Mary White, widow of the 5th Baron Abinger], and the two little Mlles. [Marie and Justine] Gobinot, all of whom did the most glorious work.

The hospital was a slaughterhouse. . . . I finally went to a wounded captain, who, seeing the chaos, sent for surgeons and men to come in at once. Then the Red Cross came and a rolling canteen. One English nurse arrived; she had lost her formation and had walked miles to get here. It seemed as if God had sent them all from Heaven!

Mrs. Hammond [possibly Miss May Hammond, a member of the Smith College Canteen], [nurse] Mary Peyton, and an American trained nurse, Miss [Lilian] Wyles [later a Scotland Yard chief inspector], all came in and helped too wonderfully for words. The new équipe [team] that arrived was splendid, and its head surgeon, Major [Jacques] Le Grand, was a most marvelous operator. We took all cases we could save to the operating room; the others we had to leave in the courtyard to die like heroes, alone.

We had many English and Americans among them, and they are buried here in the garden. I have put the Stars and Stripes over our American dead. The Red Cross was splendid. They went to Paris and brought out in trucks everything we needed.

All the surgical supplies that I could save from those you sent me from the Westchester County [NY] Red Cross I had put away for emergency, and thank God for them at that horrible moment! I don't know what we would have done without them.

Hoytie W[i]borg did such splendid work. She never had her clothes off for nights, and you will probably see her in a moving picture, taken at the station here, where she and Mary Peyton and Mrs. Hammond were cheering and caring for 600 wounded. I could not be there, for as infirmière Major I had to be here as head of everything.

* * *

I had in between times to see that the surgeons had everything they needed, and from every side everyone calling for help. Through it all, I was up every morning at 4 and never got to bed till midnight. All this, while cannon was roaring, star shells exploding, bombs dropping around us—but nothing touching us, thank God!

For eight days we were in a seething hell. Oh, how gloriously our men fought. The 7th Machine Gun [Battalion, 3rd Infantry Division] men were a marvel, and such a surprise to the Huns. Now they know what they have to face. The French and English are all enthusiasm over our men.

Oh, how proud I am of them! They will help to save dear France.

The spirit of our men is glorious. Two of the 7th Machine Gun men had their legs cut off, and, of course, we did not tell them at first about it. When they found it out one turned to the other and said: 'Well, your pin has gone, too, old boy.' One of their comrades came to see them, and as he left the legless men said, with tears in their eyes:

'By Gad, we're sorry we can't go back with you to fight those damn Fritzies.'

'Never mind, boys, just to look at you lying there will make us kill as many as we can.'

I can tell you they are doing it.

Montmirail is flooded with our troops and all troops. We have been obliged now to evacuate all but the chest wound patients, whose condition is too serious to move. Until the Hell Huns are forced some distance back we shall have to be now a service de santé, as they are too close to us to keep the wounded here.

I am staying right here unless the military forces me to leave, which I don't think will happen, as they will never cross the Marne! They couldn't do it the first time, in 1914, and they won't do it now. They will try for Paris by another route, but they won't succeed.

Hoytie W[i]borg has gone to Paris. She was worn out, and the change will do her good. I can't begin to tell you how wonderful she has been.

The refugees are heart-breaking. All the old people who left their homes here in 1914 have again been evacuated. It is all too awful, and, oh, when, when, will it end.

I see that dear Mrs. Richard Irvin is dead. Oh, if you were here you would realize that death is nothing. If you could see the smiles of peace on the faces of the dead heroes you would never again fear death. . . .

Hospice de St. Vincent de Paul
Montmirail, Marne, June 16, 1918
  Dearest F———:
I received your cable congratulating me on my work here, which you must have heard of through press dispatches. I have only done my bit—only just my duty—and how could one do less? Everyone worked marvelously.

Thank God the little hospital was able to save many, many lives. In the midst of such horrors one feels so utterly hopeless, as all one can do seems so little. We are now having the thing we dread most—quiet. Cannon are always roaring and boche airplanes flying over our heads every day, but this is all quiet after the hell we have been through.

We evacuated most of our wounded today and are now waiting in suspense for what is to come next, but for how long, only God knows—or when—or where—but we are ready for whatever comes.

Poor Italy is now having her turn, but as against Austria I feel sure she will hold her own.

The refugees here would simply break your heart. Three big motor trucks arrived here filled with old men and women, some of them 90 years old. They had been in their cellars for five days, and had to be carried out by force. Some brought their rabbits and chickens in bags, dead, of course, when they reached here. One old woman took her poor old husband to the pump under my windows, and tried to wash him and clean him up. He was weeping like a child, so I went down to aid and comfort them. It was heartbreaking to hear them tell of leaving their little farms and homes, where they had always lived, and with no future, nothing to look forward to. It made my heart ache.

Oh, those boche devils! . . . .

I can't understand how this wholesale murder can go on much longer.

I am sure the Crown Prince will say the new star recently discovered is a decoration from God for his father. [This may be a reference to a star (a nova) discovered by Maximilian Wolf of University of Heidelberg, reported in the 22 Feb. 1918 *New York Times.*]

Let us pray, however—joking aside—that it may be the Star of Peace, to shine on a purified world. No one realizes what this war is unless in it.

Mary Peyton, Virginia Latrobe, and Miss [Barbara] Allen, Frederick Allen's daughter, are working near here for the refugees. It is so nice, seeing them so often. Also Miss Stevenson [possibly Margaret Stevenson], a trained nurse, and a great friend of the Kennedy Tods. Hoytie W[i]borg is at present in Paris. Now, don't worry. I intend to stick to my post to the end, and if the Huns come down on us, the Red Cross will get me out in a camion. . . .

Hospice de St. Vincent de Paul
Montmirail, Marne, June 22, 1918
　　Dearest F———:

Your letter of May 28 came today, so you see news does not come quickly from home. We are cut off by rail and telegraph, and letters and cables have to go and come by army camions. I pray that by this time you have had my letters and cables.

Thank Heaven, we are still to be a French Army hospital, and not service de santé, as they intended to do when the Huns got so close. They have had a big fight over it, and Generals and Inspectors galore here to decide it.

We do not dare to keep seriously wounded now for any length of time, for no one knows when the next offensive will come.

I now know what "front line" really means. No one goes in or out except by military camion or Red Cross. No private telegrams can be sent, and, to our joy, we have no food-ration cards. Boche over our heads all day, and cannons booming. I am so used to it now I don't mind it.

I am so homesick to see you all, and my boys, but I will not leave my work until the end of this horrible war, if God continues to give me health and strength.

We now have four surgeons, and many trained infirmières. I am resting a little and waiting in suspense for the next drive, which is sure to come.

All the cleaning men here are now Italians. I give them cigarettes every night, which they adore. Poor souls! There are no blankets for them, and they sleep on the ground. I have asked Captain [David] Wheeler of the Red Cross to try to get some.

* * *

I don't believe the war will last much longer, but am fearful the German devils will offer such an advantageous peace that the Allies might be tempted to accept it.

The Huns are in a great state of anxiety over the way our men are fighting. This I know to be true. We don't take many prisoners.

* * *

. . . An American soldier fell from a truck the other day and smashed his head terribly, but he is better. I give him a real American breakfast every morning with a cup of your George Washington [instant] coffee, and, oh, how the boy enjoys it!

How terrible, Mrs. Bond Emerson's boy is killed! You are only just beginning to know what it all means. Here many families have had all their men killed.

If the German people could only know what agony the French people suffer!

Don't worry about me. I shall never leave my post. I find myself a great comfort to the United States soldiers here who don't speak a word of French, as I help them out in all sorts of ways.

The fighting is all around us, twenty kilometers away on one side and fifteen on the other, but the Red Cross keeps a camion here for immediate necessity, so we feel safe.

Crystal Waters (1887–1963)

Mezzo-soprano Crystal Waters sang for American servicemen in World War I as a YMCA entertainer. She later became a voice coach and counted among her clients studio mogul Samuel Goldwyn, CBS network head William Paley, and actress Rita Gam.

"A Singing Girl in No Man's Land:
How I 'Entertained' Our Boys during Their Battle for Thiancourt"
Sunset, Jan. 1919: 40–42

Because I am living through the most thrilling, exciting days and actions of the world's history [in September 1918] it is difficult for me to write coherently. I am still wildly excited after what has just happened to me, although I sit peacefully on my cot in my little tent, ankle-deep in mud, listening to a heavy barrage. Occasionally I skate off said cot when the two big Berthas up the hill dislocate me with their concussion. Why I should be so fortunate in every way is the eternal question of my existence. That I should be actually in this greatest of all battles is nothing short of a miracle.

I came up to this fighting front to sing for fighting men, believing they needed it more than other soldiers. There had been whispers of an "all-American" offensive to be and I wanted to sing for as many as possible before that time came. When I reached the section I found that the 2nd Division were needing entertainment. I have a soft spot in my heart for the Marines, anyway. I had been with them before, but only for a few days, and it takes a full month to "do" a division of 30,000 men. When I sang for them before, they had just come out of the trenches after being in for months and fighting the biggest battles of the world in this offensive of ours and being unmercifully cut to pieces. The day after they came out I was sent up to do my bit. I was told there would be no pianos and there was no one to go with me to help, so I went alone. They were near the line, having been pushed up for these few days. I went on Saturday and on Tuesday they evacuated for another sector. Poor laddies! They had lived such a brute life and had gone through so much that they were dazed. Their minds seemed to be at a standstill and they didn't know whether they could think or not. To hear something aesthetic was like going to heaven. They had forgotten there was such a thing as music—although they had sung lustily on their way to battle. That may seem paradoxical.

There were no "Y[MCA]" huts, of course, for being on the move the "Y" moved with them. Each fighting division has a "Y" division that sticks closer than a brother. These boys had tears in their eyes as they spoke of their "Y" men. One man, and others were like him, went over the top with the boys every time—he did stretcher bearing, and when the boys pushed so far forward that the kitchens couldn't keep up with them so they were four days without food or water, he was there with chocolate and biscuits. They told me of this "Y" man carrying a man who had both legs torn off and his gas mask was gone. A gas attack came, so the "Y" man put his on the boy. Those boys worship that man. He has had two citations but he is too modest to speak of it.

The division was scattered and groups of men were billeted in each little village of the district. The "Y" took any vacant store or room or cellar in the battered, forlorn hamlet and opened a canteen. There are so few American women that I only saw one in the whole division. None of these places was large enough for an entertainment. It had to be outdoors. In one case it was under a high thatched roof put up to shelter hay. There was a wall at one end and an empty hayrick was drawn up in front of it, decorated with boughs. That was my stage. Hundreds of boys came round. Some got up on a full hayrick at one side, others climbed up in the rafters. One boy got stuck in the acute corner of a joist and could neither get up nor down. His arms waived [*sic*] violently on one side of the beam and his legs on the other. He wriggled like a frog and we all screamed with delight—giving advice in both French and English or both—until by a Herculean effort, he righted himself. Little things are so extremely funny after the tragedy of a battle.

Most of the boys were sitting on the ground in front of me, or standing with the blue uniformed French soldiers farther back. No piano, no other entertainer to change off with. I sang many songs, and taught them new ones—and they sang for me, the first real live American girl they'd seen (only the "Y" expresses it, "An honest-to-God American girl"). But I had to sing with them, for they had lost the courage to let their voices out in that struggle of life and death.

That same evening I was driven about ten miles farther on to a place where our boys were gathered in a barnyard almost a block square, waiting for me. They were all standing. The square was *crowded*—half Sammies [U.S. servicemen] and half poilus [French infantrymen]. I stood at the top of some stone steps and went through the same performance. After half an hour an officer came up and offered to help, by making a fool of himself for their amusement. He sang a simple French song and he and the poilu acted it. It was better than any Orpheum stunt! When they finished there was a shout for "seconds." At mess, when the boys go back for a second serving, they are given that name. This time it meant that they all wanted a second serving of American songs. We kept it up until dark.

I soon discovered that there was always at least one well-to-do family in the village who had a piano and who was willing to let the fighting Sammies have a treat. Then I found a boy who could play. It was much more satisfactory to me although the boys would appreciate anything. At our first place we found a piano in the chateau. The best house in the village is called a chateau no matter how humble. So I stood at the window in the drawing room and they gathered in the courtyard.

From there we went to the field artillery. Their chaplain was willing to do anything to help, and this co-operation was an inspiration. We found another great stone court, surrounded by little stone barns and houses, their red roofs shining in the sunset glow. At one corner was the chateau. The kind French Madame was charmed to let us use her piano, but alas, the window was covered with vines. I suggested that it would be splendid if the piano were out in the court. It was immediately arranged and six huskies carried it out as if it were a toy. The open court sloped and in the center of the upper side was an ancient "porte." I regret to say that one-third of this court was covered with a pile of dirty hay and manure, but the boys played it [*sic*] with fresh sweet hay and sat on it happily. A light rain began to fall, so a rubber canopy was held over the piano by two giants, and I stood beside them, singing my head off. In the middle of a song a French peasant with three plow horses came through the "porte" and was so thunderstruck at the change in his village square—crowded with Americans in khaki, looking at an American girl singing beside a piano—that he stood petrified with his astonished beasts, right in the *middle* of my audience! It

73

was so humorous to see his jaw drop and his eyes bulge that I broke down with laughter. We all laughed, but he couldn't understand, and not until the boys shouted "Allez," "Allez," would he move.

I sang on and on, even though the horses were followed by great white oxen whose horns were locked in a bow—too phlegmatic and peaceful to turn an inquisitive glance. I sang everything I had and taught them songs and still they pleaded for more. The rain had stopped and dusk came. In spite of hostile aircraft we lit a candle at each end of the piano that one might see the music. Finally the chaplain came to my assistance by making one of the boys bring his violin. Although this fighter scratched and sawed in his untutored way, it was celestial music to the boys. They sat spell bound in the darkness. He had to play his whole repertoire before they were satisfied. Then I had to sing some more and it was only the chaplain's funny story that tactfully persuaded them to see how insatiable they all were.

It is perfectly useless to try to say how enthusiastic they are and how they appreciate what we do. I shall never again endure the patting of hands of the usual American audience. I love the applause of these Americans, the howls and whistles that come with the crashing together of great strong palms. And for the first time in my life I feel that I am a necessity in this world. There is no feeling more glorious! I didn't know our boys could long so for us. But it is not for our singing alone. Really, the chief thing for an American woman to have over here is a pair of ears. How they love to talk to an American woman—it's pathetic. They have such wonderful stories to tell and they simply crave to tell them to a girl from home. If they haven't been to the front, they want to talk of their sweethearts at home, or their homes and mothers or their trip over—anything, but they *must* talk. . . .

Every evening, and almost every afternoon, I'd climbed up on a big truck that carried a piano and we would roll off to a village. With the truck against a wall and the sides down we looked like quack medicine vendors. The boys would gather around and we only needed to pass the hat to make a complete picture. The rides home, in the blackness, over strange roads (for no lights were allowed up here) were hair raising. I was always sure we were going to kill a few hundred men. The road would seem perfectly clear and suddenly we would miss a troop of soldiers on the march by two inches! One night we were nearly killed, but we weren't, so I won't take time to describe it. I went up on a Wednesday and the following Tuesday they began moving up. We supposed (although no one knew anything) that it was for the great drive.

Suddenly, all singing and entertaining seemed beside the point. I had wanted to sing for fighting men and fighting men were going into the big drive where they had no time to listen. One of my girl friends was with the division and she told me of her work in the field hospitals at Soissons. That was what I wanted to do! I begged to stay with the division and do that, but no, I was not allowed to, for I was an entertainer and couldn't just change any time I felt like it to anything I felt like doing. If I were allowed to change work I must do it for a division that might need me more than the 2nd, who had three women as it was. I was disappointed. But "C'est la guerre," and back I went. My chief had a talk with me, expressing his regret, and put me off by saying he would go to Paris to see about it. I gave up hope. There was so much moving of troops that there was no singing to be done for a night or two. I tried the first night (with the Rainbow Division [42nd Infantry Division]) out in a field, brown with khaki, but in the middle of the third song the signal was sounded and that mass of soldiers shouldered their packs and were off on the road. Back in the city I retired early—not to sleep, however. All night long the division was passing through—trucks, artillery and boys—singing at the tops of their voices. This went on the next night, too—for a division is so very large and movements can only be made at night.

The front, one finds, is always just a little beyond. The men are at the front and moving up, but there are many moves before one gets "in." When I was at Gondrecourt last winter it was the front—and one spoke of Toul with abated [sic] breath. This time the 2nd Division had moved up beyond Toul. That did seem the front.

The days of waiting were more than tiresome, but the third evening at dinner, my chief came back from Paris. I expected to go to the Rainbow Division the next day and had nothing else on my mind. Imagine my delight and astonishment when I was told I might return to the Second Division for the Drive! It was too good to be true! They said because of my months of faithful work without a leave I might do as I liked! Whoop la!

The next afternoon a motor came down and we (the two men with me) were taken 'way up beyond Toul. Still it wasn't the front although the big guns were back of us. We were located on a deserted farm. The house was too small to use but the barn was just the thing. Oh! If you could have seen it! We four girls were in a loft and the men scattered around in the stables. There was great bustle in the air. The drive was coming. When, no one knew, but we lived from one minute to the next. The men strained every muscle unloading cars of chocolate, cigarettes, cigars, tobacco—bringing them by trucks to the barn where it was sorted and taken to the outfits. We girls worked at office work. Over $25,000 was sent home by the boys in small amounts just before going in. The "Y" does not charge exchange but there is much red tape.

I got to the farm Saturday night. Monday men were dropping in to say they were going up that night. Wednesday the 11th we were asked to be ready for hospital work early the next morning. We were to get up at four and pack our bed rolls. The strain was intense but there was a calm determination. You, in the peaceful States cannot, and never will know the hatred we who are here, have for the boche. I lay in my cot that night thinking about it and before I realized it was time, the barrage began. We were only about four miles from the front and that was the biggest barrage that had ever been put over. It was like a gigantic fourth of July! From then on (one o'clock) there was not one moment of peace—just incessant shell fire. At four we got up. It was still dark, but that side of the sky was ablaze—like sheet lightning. At five the boys went over the top! We were packed in a motor and started for the field hospital just at the front. Two girls were sent to No. 1 and two to 16 and 23. There were no Red Cross nurses there, no women at all—this first line of hospitals is only for sorting the wounded and operating if an operation must be immediate. The aid stations are with the men, where the doctor and chaplain (and "Y" men often) carry them in, give first aid and dope them. The ambulance men bring them to the field hospital, where they are sorted—from there they go to evacuation hospital, and then, in hospital trains, to base hospitals. Now these men, brought in, have had nothing to eat; they are wet and cold, etc. I was there to give hot chocolate or coffee, sandwiches, etc.

It was gray dawn when I arrived on the hill. The doctors were moving about the tents and everything was ready. No wounded had arrived. We stood on the edge of that hill looking down on the battle. No Napoleon could have had a better position. We were inside the line of our balloons—the artillery were camouflaged in the woods and fields not 500 yards away—we could see the explosions of the shells on the hill opposite where fires were started and air planes were flying back and forth over the lines like swallows. I couldn't make myself realize what I was seeing—it was a dream, and yet I knew it was the greatest day the world had known. We Americans—you and we—had left no stone unturned to make this first purely American drive a success. The surprising part was that no shells were being sent back to us—only a few had been sent when the boys started over. By 8 o'clock the ambulances began coming in and from that moment I worked as fast as a machine-gun. I have never in my wildest imaginations dreamed of such a spirit among the boys. Many were severely wounded but none lost that spirit. I wasn't at all sure that I would be able to stand the strain—seeing our boys shot to pieces! Where the strength came from I cannot comprehend, but to be in such a service at such a time meant the climax of my life. Considering the offensive, we figured we'd lose 100,000 men (the end is not yet)—we had very slight losses. A few were killed as they went over the top, some were brought in unconscious and were hurried into inner rooms for operations or to die, others had their faces so shot away that it was only with a medicine dropper that I got a little water to them—but the majority were leg or arm wounds. I went with the hot drink and the rubber tube or held a sandwich for them to eat, and finally put a cigarette in their mouths and lit it. Oh, how they appreciated it! I was the only woman (the other was taken away). When I could, I'd wash the clotted blood and mud from their hands and faces. Fortunately it had rained for days previously, so the Germans could not see us prepare, but it meant the boys had to stand knee deep in water all night—and they'd had nothing to eat.

To analyze my feelings and those of the boys is my object, and yet, at that distance, it will be such a horror that you'll think I am inaccurate. We suffer in our living conditions—we hate being away from you, we hate to have our friends killed and wounded—but oh, how we appreciate the privilege of being in this fight! There was not one groan from those boys, not a complaint—except from the few who were hit before they went over the top. Then it was only that they didn't get over. One lad was frightfully hurt but he only said over and over again, "Oh, I didn't get over the top!"

Eyes would twinkle and they'd say "Gosh, they gave a good barrage!" or, "Oh, if I could have gone on, I didn't want to quit!" They'd eagerly and anxiously ask about their officers. One lieutenant was brought in with his right hand gone and his legs shot, but he insisted on sitting up for his chocolate and telling me about it. He was so grateful to be there at all, he considered himself lucky! By afternoon there were only a few brought in—some German wounded, but they looked so pathetic I fed them, too.

Up here, further up, we have a huge tent, about eighty feet long, for a warehouse, and the men and we girls have a little tent. The floor is mud and water. The town is evacuated and terribly messed up. We eat with a mess kit, with some soldiers, hospital men and signal corp [sic]. They cook in a shattered barn and we sit on a bombarded wall. Just up on the hill are two 12-inch railroad guns that shoot right into Metz—thirty miles away. They shoot at the same time and the concussion nearly tears our souls from our bodies. The offensive began Thursday. That day I was in the hospital. Friday, praise God, there were not enough wounded to keep us busy! We were ready to work all night. So we went up to the next village that had been on the line and opened a canteen. The town was shot beyond recognition but the soldiers concocted a stove of bricks and built a fire on the floor of what had been a house. All day and until midnight we served hot chocolate and gave away candy and milk chocolate. The line of men was two blocks long!

In the morning the hospitals were moving over into the city we had taken, Thiancourt, and we packed up to go over and help. Then came the experience of a thousand life times. We three girls—no other women at all—were crossing No Man's Land and going over into country held by the enemy four years—and within thirty-six hours from the time it was taken!

It was easier said than done. The road across No Man's Land was just wide enough for single file. It was shell shot and muddy. We could only go a few feet at a time, for the road was jammed with camions of ammunition following the boys—supplies of all kinds, heavy and light artillery, field kitchens, everything that could be needed for an advanced position. There was such congestion that we'd move a car length and wait half an hour or more. Some of the boys on the trucks knew me and begged for a song. I stood up on the bank at the side of the road and went to it. No Man's Land was a ravine. The Germans had been on one hill and the Americans on the other. The road led down through what had been a village now about one hundred yards from where I stood. There was not one wall standing! Each side of the road was a mass of barbed wire. In front of me was a 16-inch camouflaged cannon and on this hundreds of boys were sitting listening to me. Shells were whistling over our heads.

I couldn't realize what I was going through. It seemed as though I were in a trance!

Then we were moving again. Everywhere along the road the boys were so astonished at seeing a girl that they whooped. We went so slowly that I could see their names on their gas masks and I'd say "Hello, Mr. Donovan," etc., just to see their jaws drop. I never saw so many men at one time in my life! All America was on or beside that road as we pushed over on ground held by Germans for four years. German signs, German dugouts! But the Germans had fled. As we went down the road leading into Thiancourt we came into shell fire. Four German balloons were watching that road and directing their artillery. Once in the city we were informed we had to go back, that the boches were shelling time out of the place and there were so few wounded there was little to do. I hadn't been there three minutes before there was a whiz, bang, and a lad came running to me with a piece of hot shrapnel.

We hated to go back, of course, but we were only too glad there was so little to do in the hospitals. The next night our division began moving out and we made hot chocolate in the dark—German planes always over our heads made lights impossible—and poured it for the boys as they passed. We had so little water that the supply was limited, so we began to give hard candy and cigarettes. It cost the "Y" just $25,000 to give what it did to our division up there.

Most of last week I spent in a hut in the woods where our infantry were hidden. We made chocolate and ran a canteen, gave out pounds and pounds of writing paper and envelopes and had a concert each night. Now we're back in Toul and oh, boy, oh joy, where do we go from here? My chief claims me tomorrow for regular concert work and having been in one actual battle, I should be satisfied.

Enid Bland Yandell (1869–1934)

Born in Louisville, Kentucky, sculptor Enid Bland Yandell was the daughter of physician Lunsford Pitts Yandell Jr. She earned degrees in chemistry and art from Hampton College (KY) and completed a program at the Cincinnati Art Academy. She studied in Paris with Frederick MacMonnies. In Chicago, she studied with Lorado Taft and Philip Martiny, becoming known as one of the "White Rabbits"— female sculptors who worked with Taft on sculptures for the World's Columbian Exposition of 1893. Her notable works include the statue of Daniel Boone in Louisville, the enormous statue of Pallas Athena for the 1897 Nashville Centennial Exposition, and the Carrie Brown memorial fountain in Providence, RI. She was the first female member of the National Sculpture Society and founded the Branstock School in Edgartown, MA.

During World War I she was involved with Orphelins de la Guerre, an organization devoted to the care of French children with family members in the war, and Appui aux Artistes, which provided low-cost meals in Paris for workers in the arts who had been deprived of their livelihood by the war. In addition, she served with the Red Cross in the debarkation records department in Hoboken, New Jersey. Her *New York Times* obituary of 13 June 1934 noted, "She received considerable recognition for her filing systems, which, when the war was over, made it possible to obtain the name, whereabouts and condition of every man wounded in the American Army."

"Every Child Is of Value to France"
Lecture at the home of Mrs. Robert [Grace] McGann, Chicago
November 11, 1915
Archives of American Art microfilm

. . . .I noticed a crowd around the post office and the two railroad stations, and I found out that war had been declared. And it was very remarkable how quiet everybody was—there was no panic, no excitement, but there was keen interest. It seemed to me that Paris was like a human being more than a town, and that as a human being she had received an important note and was ready for it. Then the next morning everything was busy; it was [as] if a hive of bees had been disturbed; everybody was evidently attending to his business and doing it very rapidly. . . . .And there were no complaints, even from the women with babies in their arms, the wives sent their husbands off with smiles and words of good cheer, and if there was any crying it was done at home.

Then we realized that what had happened in 1870 would happen again and that Paris would be besieged. And almost immediately there was nothing left, scarcely, in the food stores, and we had to go and stand in line and we were limited as to what we could buy; sometimes only five cents worth of sugar or butter—depended upon the number in the family. Then the police issued a notice that all foreigners must get passports or else leave. There was a great crowd in the police stations, where they were issuing numbers for our passports, similar to the way in which you get your tickets for the omnibus. We had to show something to verify the fact that we were either Americans, or Poles, or Russians, and if our papers were found satisfactory then we got our permit to stay in Paris.

. . . . I had made up my mind that France had been good to me and the least I could do was to stay and help, my friends in this country would make it possible, and I thought if I stayed on the ground I might be of benefit, and when some of my friends asked me to go home with them, I answered, "No, France for me." And it was the most wonderful experience, the most beautiful and heartbreaking of my life.

. . . . So I joined the Red Cross and applied for service among the women, children and old people. . . . . Of course all who could get out got out and all the stations were flooded with people trying to get away. Then an order was issued to close the schools and that the children should be taken out of the city. Then the question was, what to do with these children. I became interested in a bunch of about sixty little ones and while talking to a doctor who had charge of them he asked me if there was some American institution where the children could be placed. I knew that all the girls from the American girls' club had left and that the clubhouse was empty. I asked permission to put the children in there, which of course was given to me, and we got the club ready and cradles for the babies, and inside of twenty-four hours all was in readiness. During the mobilization the father of two children, whose mother was dead, a little boy of six and a little girl of nine, said to me: "I am mobilized, I am going tonight; who will take care of my children?" and without stopping to think I said: "I will take care of them." He gave them to me with their papers that each French citizen must have and his name and regiment, and I became responsible for these and ten others. Four of them slept in my studio and others in studios of friends of mine for two months, the others were with friends in Paris who offered me beds and accommodations, and I took care of them.

And then the schools were opening and I realized with the work that had developed I could not take care of these children properly and be responsible for them under the conditions. Just where to put them was the question. We were now feeding 800, who had come to us under the same conditions and I felt responsible for them, not knowing whether or not their fathers would come back. They were not orphans and could not be put into asylums, a great many of the schools had been closed and those which were open were expensive and my funds would not admit of paying for them. Then, I had taken brothers and sisters and I did not want to have the members of one family separated. Finally I was able to have them taken care of by the Université Populaire, which is more like Hull House here in Chicago than any other institution I know of, and a great many of the ordinary working people belong to it.

Then when the men who were being mobilized said where should they leave their children, we said: "We will take care of your children and we will not abandon them and we will keep you posted." The UP had collected about 150 of them and put them around in different houses that people lent to them or people took them and were only too glad to take care of them. The question was whether they were being properly fed and were they going to school? Then they divided the children into families of ten to twenty children with a house mother and an assistant and they went to school and dined in the hotel which had been engaged for the purpose, and the house mother was responsible for their bringing up, manners and character. I asked them to take my ten children down there and I took them down there with a bunch of sixty that had been collected. We went down seventy in all, and that the beginning of my special family. Some of these children had been brought by their fathers, some of them were sent to us with a tag saying, "I am going to the Université Populaire," and came through perfectly safe. Some were brought by the soldiers. There were two little Belgians picked up from the battlefield, about two and three years old, well dressed and giving every sign of having been well taken care of. When these little children were brought to the table they were so polite, but they objected to the pewter service in use, saying it must have been intended for the servants. Of course, there were many interesting incidents; there was a charming little boy, now in my family, named Rene; his father was mobilized and his mother killed during the bombardment of Reims. I have become much attached to him. The one comfort I had during those nine months of sorrow was the pleasure I got from seeing my children; they were glad to see me and for a little while I could forget the terrible conditions.

All the service is voluntary; there is no paid service. We have a thousand children with about twenty children to each house mother. We have eight trained nurses . . . . Every child is of value to France and we wanted to do all we could to save them, and we had a wonderful record. . . . Out of from seven hundred to a thousand children only one death since the war began. The nearest to an epidemic we had was contagion from the trench babies. These children are there constantly, though nobody knows how they get there, but the soldiers like them, looking upon them as mascots. But the military authorities do not want the soldiers to take care of them and so they sent us fifty of these trench babies, and . . . they had body lice. About 150 children got them, and we had an awful time washing them and getting them clean.

. . . . [T]he most interesting was to see the way these children developed. There were five that came under my special care, and I have never seen human beings look like that. I have read descriptions of children and of people who were dirty, but I never saw anything like this. These children had been left after the bombardment and had lived in a dog kennel. . . . They had become wild and would bite and scratch. Two women devoted themselves to the children for two weeks before they were clean. But when I came away they had all grown from four to five inches and did not look like the same children. They had stopped biting each other and stopped fighting.

There is one absolute law at the Université Populaire, that no one must strike a child for any reason and if any grown person does this they are summarily dismissed. They are governed and controlled entirely by love. . . . Most of them can be corrected by simply not kissing them at night, and if that does not appeal to them we cut off dessert. . . .

. . . .[Y]ou have heard of the men who have lost their minds in the trenches, and there are a great many of them. I know one young sculptor who has come back from the front, who is at times quiet but at other times violently insane. The sufferings of the horses and dogs were what affected him most—the cries of the horses and dogs that are wounded—and he tries to help these animals.

Then there are many who come back from the front completely disabled—paralyzed—but not wounded, simply broken in health from the awful life they have lived, and these seem to me the saddest of all. They have not had the glory of shedding their blood for their country, but they are broken and useless and not fit for anything because of the terrible hardships in the trenches.

"An Interpreter of Army Life"

From "Chicago Tribune Army Edition Notes Arrival in Paris of Miss Peggy Hull,"
El Paso Morning Times 17 Jul 1917: 1.

Harriet Chalmers Adams (1875–1937)

Harriet Chalmers Adams, ca. 1908-19. Library of Congress, Prints and Photographs Division, reproduction no. LC-DIG-npcc-19900.

Born in Stockton, CA, Harriet Chalmers Adams became a celebrated explorer of places such as Africa, Asia, Cuba, Haiti, and Latin America. She lectured and wrote about her travels, illustrating these with her own photographs. In 1899 she married Franklin Pierce Adams, an engineer who served in various positions at the Pan American Union (later the Organization of American States). During World War I, she was a correspondent in France for *National Geographic*. In 1926 she was elected the first president of the Society of Woman Geographers.

Elizabeth Foxwell

"Luneville Feels Crushing Hand of Hun Invader"

National Geographic Nov.–Dec. 1917. Repr. *Berkeley Daily Gazette*, 2 Mar 1918: 3

...Luneville is a gray, industrial town of 20,000 souls, in French Lorraine, prospering before the war in its manufacture of railway carriages and motor cards, chinaware and chemical salts. A gorgeous chateau is all that remains of its former glory, when the dukes of Lorraine made it their playground. In their day this palace was gayer than Versailles, and its gardens were noted throughout Europe, serving Watteau's pupils as a model when they painted the gorgeous fetes of the Far East. The chateau is now occupied by the mayor, M. Keller, who played an important role during the German invasion of the town.

Madame Mirman motored us out to Luneville. Although she is the wife of [Léon Mirman], the prefect of this whole department [Meurthe and Moselle] and is known by sight to every sentinel on the road, the automobile was halted every quarter of an hour for inspection of passports and information as to where we were bound.

Women in Fields

In the fields women were mowing hay. I was reminded of a woman I had seen near Rheims. A shell struck a near-by haystack, but she kept on mowing.

We ascended a tortuous road to the summit of the hill of Leomont, where a decisive battle had been fought. This was a most comprehensive view back over the plain of Nancy, north and east over the French front. In a hollow, at our feet, lay a ruined village which is now being restored through the generosity of a group of wealthy Californians.

From this hill to the one opposite the battle had raged. We picked up fragments of French and German shells and the soldier-chauffeur explained which was which, one being bluer than the other. There were many graves on this hill, and above one I saw a soldier's tattered cap hanging on the little white cross.

"I placed it there over two years ago," Madame Mirman said, "when I came out with my husband. He buried the dead. We did not know the boys' names, but we marked each cross with the number of the regiment wherever we could."

Flowers on Graves

On the graves wildflowers were blooming—red poppies, blue cornflowers, white daisies. Even in death, nature in France greets her soldiers with the tricolor.

Luneville shows the hoofmarks of the Hun, those terrible twenty days when the enemy was master of the city. The town hall and prefecture were destroyed, the industrial section burned, shops pillaged, homes looted, men and women murdered. Cultured people, like the Kellers, tell the story quietly, but their eyes have a dangerous gleam. "I would gladly have given my life," the mayor said, "if I could have spared my fellow-citizens those horrible atrocities."

Unarmed men fired on; an old woman run through with a bayonet; a mother driven insane at seeing her son stabbed and her daughter carried off by drunken soldiers—such stories are so common in the foothill towns of the Vosges that the very air is polluted. The birds in the chateau garden have almost forgotten how to sing since the Prussians passed that way.

Harriet Chalmers Adams in Rheims, France, ca. 1917. From left: French officer, Chalmers Adams, lawyer Paul Cravath, Capt. Paul Dumas, unidentified man, journalist Charles Edward Russell, unidentified man, Judge Robert Grant. Library of Congress, Prints and Photographs Division, reproduction no. LC-DIG-hec-02850.

Leola Allard (1881–1951)

Leola Allard. From the Chicago Examiner, *12 May 1917, p. 5.*

In 1903, Leola Allard became the first female editor of *The Northwestern*, a student periodical at Northwestern University. She served as women's page editor for the *Chicago Daily News* and the *Pittsburgh Post-Gazette*. During her career she also wrote for the *Chicago Tribune* and was a columnist for King Features. Allard married Fred L. Day in October 1920.

As a reporter for the *Chicago Examiner* during World War I, she wrote some short "slice-of-life" pieces about Camp Grant in Rockford, IL.

Elizabeth Foxwell

"The Idol of the Camp"
From "Unofficial 'Mother' Adopts Officers at Rockford Camp"
Chicago Examiner 10 Sept. 1917: 4

Camp Grant, Rockford, Ill. Sept. 9—It wasn't like any other Sunday dinner party I ever attended. It was better.

They call it "officers' mess," and the food put other meals to shame. It was in the camp at the edge of Rock River, where the First Illinois Engineers, Company A, are quartered.

Until Saturday a frame covered with white mosquito netting was the mess tent. But the weather is getting much colder—too cold for the idol of the camp, the beautiful, snowy-haired mother of Captain C. C. Saner.

So a white frame house nearby was moved, and to-day meals were served there.

Mrs. Ida M. Saner oversees the officers' mess, unobtrusively mothers all its members. They love her.

Corps' Only Mother
The widow of a soldier, she is the only mother at the cantonment, and an ideal one to take all "her boys" under her care.

"I came here to be with my son," said Mrs. Saner. "But one by one the other officers wanted to come in and make it a sort of family. Now there are a dozen of us together. I am very happy."

At the dinner table were Major D. H. Sawyer, construction quartermaster, who really made Camp Grant; Captain C. W. Noble, Captain E. G. Thomas, Captain W. T. Charles, Captain F. B. Laramie, Lieutenant W. H. Dean, Captain A. L. Nelson, Captain A. M. Garwood, Captain D. L. Vanaukin, Captain C. C. Saner and the wife of Sergeant Leroy Paul.

The real live topic at dinner was a groundhog eaten by Captains Charles and Garwood. It was captured in the rifle range and stuffed by the cook for those who were bold enough to partake.

Laughter greeted the departure of Major Sawyer, who, the officers declared, probably was going for the ambulance to haul away the two captains.

It was the "fillingest" meal soldiers could eat.

Eighty milk-fed chickens were roasted yesterday in this corner of camp. The mashed potatoes were flaky and the gravy was browned and had chopped green olives in it, in plentiful quantity.

Eat Elderberry Pie

There was jelly and coleslaw with an olive oil dressing, and best of all elderberry pie, made by Mrs. Saner, from berries the soldiers picked.

"They aren't very good this year," she said. "They are too green." But the pie disappeared hurriedly.

It was suggested a piece be sent to General [Thomas H.] Barry. For his sake, I hope it was.

After dinner, when I started for home, the piano player in the mess tent of the private soldiers was going merrily. A lot of gay colors were about. Visitors' day! Purple and red hats lighted the camp, which had looked uniformly olive drab. And in the tents many soldiers were writing home.

Nellie Bly (Elizabeth Cochrane Seaman)
(1864–1922)

Nellie Bly, aka Elizabeth Cochrane Seaman, ca. 1890. Library of Congress, Prints and Photographs Division, reproduction no. LC-USZ62-75620.

Elizabeth Jane Cochran was born on May 5, 1864, in Cochran's Mills, PA, a town founded by her father, a judge. She added an "e" to her surname as a teenager. At age sixteen she became the *Pittsburgh Dispatch*'s first female reporter. In April 1895 she married sixty-eight-year-old Robert Seaman, wealthy owner of the Ironclad Manufacturing Co., and much of her life was consumed after her husband's death in 1904 by lawsuits against embezzling employees and family members.

A groundbreaking "stunt" journalist for Joseph Pulitzer's *New York World*, she had herself committed to an asylum so she could write about the treatment of the mentally ill (later published as *Ten Days in a Mad-House*, 1887). In 1889 she undertook a celebrated around-the-world trip for the *World*, beating by eight days Phineas Fogg's eighty-day journey in Jules Verne's novel (later published as *Nellie Bly's Book: Around the World in Seventy-Two Days*, 1890).

During World War I, she covered the war in Central Europe for the *New York Evening Journal*. As she wrote some pieces seeking relief for Austria—an eventual U.S. enemy—government officials questioned her upon her return to the United States. After she died in 1922 from pneumonia, neither her *New York Times* nor *Washington Post* obituary mentioned a word about her World War I reporting.

"A Mixture of Senseless Human Beings"
From "Nelly [sic] Bly in Trenches—Die Like Flies of Cholera—Men Kill Unseen Enemy"
Washington Herald, 8 Dec. 1914: 3

By Nellie Bly
("America's Greatest Newspaper Woman and Herald Correspondent")

Prsemaryl, Galicia [probably Przemysl, part of the Kingdom of Galicia and Lodomeria then situated between Poland and Russia], Oct. 30 (by mail)—Long, deep trenches connected one line of caves with another line in advance.

Over the front line branches of trees had been stuck in the earth.

It looked like stubby growth or scrub wood. It concealed the caves completely.

Soldiers were busy bringing the branches from a grove on the hill when the burring of an aeroplane made the captain give them a quick order to stop and stand still.

The aeroplane came over our heads like a giant snake feeder in the air. No one knew whether it was friend or foe. The strongest glasses used by our officers did not help us.

One officer said it was a German aeroplane; another thought it was Russian. We could take our choice.

Some one suggested to look out for a bomb, but none fell. The aeroplane went straight over toward the Russian army until it was lost to view. In the middle of the battery was one straw-lined cave. It stood alone. Before it stood the commander-in-chief.

Within the cave, resting on a bed of straw, was the most important man of the outfit.

The Cholera Huts

A telephone was strapped to him. Over each ear was a receiver, strapped to his breast a transmitter.

The familiar buzzing and the operator repeated in loud tones what he heard. The commander introduced the soldiers back to their branch bearing labor.

On we went. [A] group of a dozen hovels lining each side of the road caught our attention. On each gale post, if I may call it so, for a woven fence of tree branches protected the houses from the road, were tacked white cards.

On straw, only bits of straw at that, along the sides of these miserable, filthy hovels huddled human forms in blood-stained, muddy uniforms. Around the doorways, in the stable, everywhere they lay, heedless, inanimate, motionless.

Dirty women and children opened their doors to look at us. The men lying on the wisps of dirty straw around the sides of their hovels did not seem to interest them. Yet they appeared not cruel. They looked curiously at the men, but when they looked at me they slowly smiled kindly and friendly.

Turning my back to one horror, turned my face to another. Between a hovel and a barn an open space about 6 by 6 had been loosely boarded up at one side, the hovel and barn forming the other two sides. The fourth was open.

Die Like Flies

On the ground was strewn straw. In that straw was a mixture of senseless human beings, knapsacks, flasks, discarded bloody bandages, a gun and other unspeakables.

One motionless creature had his cap on his head. He had a short, stubby brown beard. Great black circles were around his sunken eyes. Black hollows were around his nose and his ears were black. Still he lived. Dying, I believe.

Near him, completely covered by his coat, was a form. Occasionally it shivered convulsively. That was all.

Beside him sat a soldier, his chin on his breast. Some one shoved him and yelled at him. He tried to lift his head. Useless. It sank again, his chin against his breast. Cholera, the posts were marked, dear friends. Human creatures they were, lying there in a manner our health authorities would prohibit for hogs or the meanest beasts.

Kill Unseen Enemy

The constant singing of the Russian shells over our heads was like the sound of huge skyrockets as they ascend. There is no explosion, however. I could scarcely realize they brought death. But when they strike death and destruction are the result.

A few steps from the cholera hovels is the battery. I ran to it in delight.

Shot after shot was fired, each gun in turn, but though I watched with the greatest care I saw nothing but a bit of brown stuff like paper fall to earth again.

Whom they killed, what they killed, they knew not. The order comes to fire in a certain direction and a specified distance. "Three hundred and forty metres," I heard them say, again.

Thus men kill without emotion. They do not witness the result, and so the killing is less hard.

"A Scourge Sweeping the World"
From "Woman Writer Describes Trip on Hospital Train"
Washington Herald 13 Jan. 1915: 5

En route to Budapest, Nov. 3 [1914]—. . . . Every moment had its new interest. The trains we met, filled with happy, confident soldiers in new, fresh uniforms, their cars decorated with the Austrian and Hungarian colors and branches from pine trees, made my throat contract. Fine looking, healthy, frank-eyed, splendid fellows, all just at the early threshold of manhood.

With flowers in their military caps and songs upon their lips; with faith and confidence in the justice of their cause; with a love for all mankind, but convinced, like the first Christians, of the righteousness of their cause; they go joyfully into the hell of battle. The trains, long and lime-splattered, which lay alongside to let us pass, or which pass us as we went, tell the next story.

The flowers, dried and faded, still remain in their mud-stained caps. Their eyes are sunken and haunted by the vision of the most frightful hell living man ever witnessed. Their lips have forgotten how to smile. Their bodies bear wounds. They are sore and filled with the pain of long days and endless nights in wet, cold, muddy trenches. Besides their frightful wounds, they have cholera, dysentery, typhoid and hollow coughs which rack them like the last cough of a consumptive.

Of ammunition and supplies there seems no scarcity. Long trains bearing cannons, blankets, wagons and ammunition never end. They are everywhere, on the rail and roads. When I got up at daylight we were running parallel with a road. The road was lined with wagons. I counted 500 and gave it up. When our train finally took a different course, I saw, quite a long while after, an end of part of that caravan winding between two hills.

Clocks Everywhere

I notice the clocks are going. I would know by this alone that we are out of Galicia. There are clocks everywhere in Galicia. On the walls, on tables, on stairways, on buildings. I even found one under my bed in Sanok. I am convinced the natives like the look of clocks. There must be something in the white face with its twelve Roman figures especially fascinating to them. Otherwise they would not buy them. For not a clock in all Galicia goes, not even the clocks in the stations.

In Hungary they make their clocks work. The beautiful landscape, the well-tilled fields, the busy, prosperous-looking people, the seemingly good roads all tell a different story.

No longer can I tell the story of filth everywhere. Truly the railways are abominable, but at every station a large force is busy with lime and brooms. Women in short, full skirts and high boots, the type made familiar to us by [Franz] Lehar's popular opera, are doing most of the work. Cholera may be in their midst, but these energetic people will fight it every inch of the way.

I forgot to say that Prince Croy's train is Zug Lit D. It is one of six trains fitted out and maintained by the Knights of the Maltese Cross. They are independent of all other societies, and their members maintain these trains.

Pleased the Kaiser

"We have made such a record," said Prince Croy to me, "that the German Emperor has asked us to establish a branch of our society in Germany."

Wednesday, Nov. 4.—Three soldiers died in Prince Croy's train last night. Once the thought of three deaths on one's train in one night would have been appalling, but here, where death is everywhere, where the sight of dead and dying men is as familiar to one as sparrows in New York, one gets hopeless, not heartless. It is like a scourge sweeping the world. One stands dumb, despairing, dry-eyed before the vastness of the misery.

Prince Croy fed us twice again from his splendid kitchen. Without him we should have had to exist on our biscuits. We stop continually, but not where we can obtain food. Indeed, the small, lime-covered stations we have passed are not inviting. . . .

Thursday, Nov. 5—. . . . We breakfasted in a station with a lot of officers, who watched us with interest. We had tea with rum rolls, or light bread, the first I have seen in Europe, and two boiled eggs. One of mine was fresh. Some had worse luck, others better. Prince Croy lost two more soldiers by death last night. That is five out of 130.

Remarkable Recoveries

"I have had soldiers frightfully wounded," Prince Croy told me, "who have made extraordinary recoveries. One man had three shots. One entered his forehead and came out at the back of his head. One entered the base of his head at the back and came out on the opposite side of the temple and one shot went through his leg. Five weeks after, when I went to see him, he jumped to his feet and saluted.

"I had another more horrible," he continued. "A man had his entire lower jaw torn off with a shrapnel. His tongue hung out on his neck and chest. He had been five days in the trenches after receiving his wounds before the firing ceased long enough to let him be carried away. He was famished. We inserted a tube in his throat. He fought vigorously, as he thought it would hurt. But we insisted and poured soup into him. The moment he felt the soup in his stomach he made frantic motions for more. He was wild for food. We could not feed him enough. Now they are making a new jaw in the hospital and he is recovering."

When Prince Croy was told how eagerly the poor fellows demanded more food, he laughed delightedly, showing how happy he felt to be able to give some comfort to the suffering.

Great strings of wild geese floating like worms in the sky mingle with the white clouds in the blue above us. Aeroplanes, whose whizzing motors warn us of their approach long before they are visible, come and go. We are left to speculate whether they are friend or foe. The strongest glass does not disclose their identity.

Many of the men carry alcohol lamps. They are always "cooking tea" as they express it. Some of the men seem to be eternally eating. At one place we stopped a ragged barefooted woman, with an old shawl wrapped around her head, stood watching our waiting train. Some of our party talked to her and finally persuaded her to go to the cluster of houses in the valley way below and get them some chickens. She returned after the long trip with four young broilers—pullets. She said they cost five kronen—$1. A man laid four kronen on the ground and grabbed the chickens. The woman protested. Either give back her chickens or give her five kronen. The man left her crying, took the chickens to the other side of the train and killed them.

Championed the Woman

The woman covered her face with her ragged shawl, crying. I had maintained a very careful attitude up to this moment, but here my sense of justice prevented my being silent. I went to the man protesting. "Either give the woman what she asks," I said, "or give back her chickens."

"She's had enough," he said, going on with his butchering.

"It is not right or fair," I urged. "If you don't give her the right amount, now that you have killed her chickens, I shall pay her."

"Give her another krone," several other men advised. He would not, but his friend did. The woman kissed my hand. Several of the men threw pebbles at her and shooed her away. Down the valley side she went, a forlorn, bare-footed figure in a ragged, faded shawl.

The men had a great feast of chicken and rice. I made my dinner on five biscuits, postage stamp size. I could only eat chicken under some conditions. This was not one of them. At any rate, I was not invited to eat.

We have no light. It is dark at 5. It gives me time to try to patch out a night's rest on the slippery edge of my compartment seat.

Madeleine Z. Doty (1877–1963)

Madeleine Z. Doty. From Society's Misfits *(1916), frontispiece.*

Born in Bayonne, NJ, Madeleine Zabriskie Doty earned a BL from Smith College in 1900, an LLB from New York University in 1902, and a PhD in international relations from the University of Geneva in 1934. She practiced law in New York before serving as secretary of the Children's Court Committee of the Russell Sage Foundation. Like Nellie Bly's investigation into mental health care, Doty lived incognito in a New York women's prison for a week to report on conditions there (discussed in her book *Society's Misfits*, 1916). She attended the 1915 Women's Peace Congress at the Hague with Jane Addams, Emily Greene Balch, and an international array of activists. In 1919 she married Roger Baldwin, the future founder of the ACLU; they divorced in 1925. She later became a teacher and the international secretary for the Women's International League for Peace and Freedom.

In summer 1916 Doty traveled to Germany to assist starving children and assess the country's wartime conditions. Her impressions were published in a series of articles from November 1916 to January 1917 in the *New York Tribune* and in her book *Short Rations* (1917).

"A New State of Affairs for Germany"
From "Half-Starved Mothers of Germany in Revolt Over
Food 'Red Tape'"
New York Tribune 3 Dec. 1916: 6

... I appealed to a woman social worker. "Very well," she said. "I'll show you what is happening." She took me to the north of Berlin. There little children swarmed, dirty, ragged, barefooted and pale. This is a new state of affairs for Germany. Heretofore there have always been at least potatoes and clothes. No one has gone hungry. Paternalism flourishes only when the family is fed. When father fails to furnish food the children rebel. The spirit of rebellion is abroad in Germany.

We visited several tenements. The following is a typical family. A mother, nine children and grandmother, two rooms and a kitchen. Father in the war; income 144 marks ($38 a month; rent $7 a month). This mother could not afford to eat at a feeding kitchen. One meal at 10 cents a head meant $1.20. The baby was six months old. It has what is termed "English krankheit [disease]." It was weak from lack of nourishment. It could not raise its arms. Since September 1 only children under six are allowed milk. The allowance is a pint a day. Not enough to nourish a baby. This family was living on tea and potatoes.

We visited many families. I could not admire my companion. She was very proud, but tears ran down her cheeks. She belonged to the official class. She adored Germany and held every German act right, yet her heart bled for her people. Vainly she was trying to stem the tide. She dashed her tears aside to say:

"Do you wonder Germany women are bitter? But England shall not bring us to our knees, rather we will give our last baby first."

....[A] reliable and well-informed Social Democrat told me that in the babies' hospital the increase in mortality was 50 percent. I consulted Dr. [Ludwig] Kimmle, the head of the German Red Cross in Berlin, about the milk supply. He thought the best investment goats. More money had come from the Christian Work Fund and I turned over 4,000 marks (owing to depreciation only about $800) to him to buy goats for the north of Berlin. The wealthy agrarian who sold the goats asked 150 marks ($37.50) a goat. Ordinarily the price is thirty marks, or $5.50, per goat. Was this German agrarian patriotic or efficient? He made money out of the German babies' necessity. Why did the government permit it? Was it efficient? Does Germany handle its food supply efficiently?

. . . . I asked the Social Democrats about the food riots. They occurred, I was told, chiefly in the spring, when the potatoes gave out. In Hamburg the women ran straight on the solders' bayonets in the struggle for food and several were killed. The following day, Sunday, the government had to throw open the Hamburg provision stores and let the people buy, to restore peace. Berlin has had several riots. In some cities women have been shot. "It is quite easy to start a rebellion," said a Social Democrat to me. "Several times we went to the market and urged the crowd to riot. But we stopped, for women were put in prison and the children left destitute."

But when there are no potatoes there will be a riot. As long as there is food for the children, however inadequate, the women keep quiet. Their hearts are sore, but they dare not rebel. They fear the fate that may befall their husbands at the front if they make trouble. Or, if the husband is wounded, they fear he will not be well cared for. Or they fear their children may be taken from them. But these women when spoken to look wise and say: "Wait until our men come back; then you'll see."

Peggy Hull (1889–1967)
(Henrietta Eleanor Goodnough Hull Kinley Deuell)

Peggy Hull, 1931. Library of Congress, Prints and Photographs Division, reproduction no. LC-USZ62-127286.

Born in Kansas, Peggy Hull began her journalism career at the Junction City [KS] *Sentinel* and worked at newspapers in states such as California, Colorado, and Minnesota. When she covered National Guard troops patrolling the U.S.-Mexico border in the wake of Mexican bandit Pancho Villa, she became acquainted with General "Black Jack" Pershing. This relationship assisted her when she persuaded the *El Paso Morning Times* to send her to France in 1917; Pershing's support enabled her to stay at a U.S. artillery training camp for 6 weeks, despite her lack of accreditation from the War Department. This special access caused male correspondents to move for her recall to Paris and thus placed constraints on her as to what she could cover. She returned to the United States in December 1917, achieved official accreditation, and covered the AEF troops sent to

Siberia in winter-spring 1919 as a correspondent for the Newspaper Enterprise Association and the *Evening Independent*.

Hull was married three times; her third husband was New York *Daily News* editor Harvey Deuell. Her articles from WWI France for the *El Paso Morning Times* were not bylined but usually had "Peggy" in the headline and ended with her signed first name, suggesting that her relationship with the paper's readership was close enough to make her surname superfluous. Her return from France was ballyhooed in the December 24, 1917, headline "Peggy Is Home!".

"Peggy in Paris Describes Her First Terrorizing Experience with Murderous German Planes"
El Paso Morning Times 2 Sept. 1917: 7.

Paris—"But love such as ours"—I had just gotten this far in an impassioned love story and was turning the page when a long, shivering shriek arose from the street below. It was followed by the grating, coarse sounds of many automobile horns, and I could hear machines speeding down the Rue de Rivoli. I had gone to bed and turned out all my lights with the exception of the rose-colored reading lamp on the little stand by my table. There was such an atmosphere of peace and rest in the shadowy pink depths of my room that I leisurely turned my page and once more became submerged in the love story.

* * *

"It's just a fire," I said to myself, and from long experience as a newspaper woman, I knew almost any kind of a love story can be more interesting than the average fire.

The sirens kept wailing and the automobiles clanking their hideous horns. I read on. The noise died down and I could hear the whirring of aeroplanes. But aeroplanes whir all night and all day long—they have become almost as common as the clanging of street cars. And, besides, the lovers in the story were having their first quarrel.

* * *

There came a short, quick bang on my white door. I sat up rather quickly and recalled that over an hour ago I had rung for the waiter. Very often it takes the waiter that long to respond and any lack of service is always explained by the suave manager in the same words, "C'est la guerre" ("it is the war").

Before I could reach the door there came another sharp, impatient rap, and I opened it to find a little Frenchman waving his arms and talking very fast—I looked at him blankly. My stare seemed to excite him—he talked louder and faster and waved his arms furiously—then he looked at me quite disgusted—reached his hand around the door—snapped out the light—and walked away, leaving me standing in a pitch-dark room. I knew something was wrong, and a helpless, infantile feeling came over me, for I could not call him back and find out what had happened.

* * *

Other Frenchmen hurried through the hall and as they passed my door I caught two words—"bosche" and "police." Then I knew—very suddenly why the aeroplanes were humming over the hotel courtyard—why my light had been snapped out. I was going through my first air raid experience.

When I was a little girl thunder terrorized me. If mother wasn't with me, I remember I used to crawl under the bed or into a dark closet. Tonight the old fear came back but tonight I was alone in a strange land of blackness. There were no mother's arms to flee to—no one to even say—at least so that I could understand it—a reassuring word. I felt my way back to my bed and climbed under the red satin quilt—I piled a great pillow on top of my head and waited.

* * *

I thought of El Paso and the quiet summer nights back there—I thought of the wonderful park in Versailles which I had just visited—the wide forests so still and peaceful under the starlit sky. I thought of England and its placid countryside—its dreamy cows and flowered meadows—its lanes made for lovers—the most beautiful world our imaginations could conjure—turned into hell—filled with unknown and unexpected horrors by the maddened kaiser-crazy Germans.

* * *

You'll probably read this story at the breakfast table while you're sipping your good coffee, just as you have read many similar stories on other air raids. You'll say, "That's pretty bad," as you lay the paper down and hurry off to work—but the full meaning of an air attack can never be comprehended unless one of the bombs falls outside your window. Yet for three years these people had lived in hourly dread—have seen their worst premonitions fulfilled—and I, trembling beneath my scarlet coverlet, knew for the first time what war from the sky spelled in emotions.

People kept hurrying up and down the hall—talking in frightened voices—arguing, chattering, intense. My refuge offered little comfort. I slipped out of bed—groped around and found a dressing gown and slippers and joined the throngs outside. They were all going to the roof. I followed.

A significant silence fell upon each person as the heavens came into full view. Banked against the north horizon were a flotilla of aeroplanes—shooting and streaking back and forth across the sky like great stars. Their broad searchlights banded the firmament—they criss-crossed and circled, while the French observatory lamp threw a wide path of electric sunshine across their courses. Coney Island would spend a million dollars to reproduce that spectacle.

* * *

The entire air defense of Paris had been turned out and their combined guide lamps turned the light of day over the capital city. The earth was forgotten. I looked down and nothing but clinging blackness was all around. The blur of voices reached me faintly—otherwise there seemed to be nothing but a dark, widthless, depthless space below me. Every light had been extinguished. Then I looked at the white sky and wanted to laugh! What chance had even a fleet of enemy planes against that marvelous, swiftly moving formation out there which had taken over the entire horizon—what chance to drop even a tiny bomb on the outskirts when those guardian birds swarmed with dizzying speed across the whole expanse of sky?

Lights flashed up from the streets near by and startled my eyes. Then from a neighboring avenue came the triumphant, exulting song of a bugle. The danger was over! The enemy planes had fled back to their own lines and I went slowly to my room, with the sweet tones of the final signal lingering in my ears.

Alice Rohe (1876–1957)

Alice Rohe, ca. 1925. Library of Congress, Prints and Photographs Division, reproduction no. LC-DIG-ppmsca-32096

Born in Lawrence, KS, Alice Rohe earned her BA from the University of Kansas in 1896 and supported women's suffrage. Her brother-in-law was Roy W. Howard, head of the Scripps-Howard chain of newspapers and editor and publisher of the *New York World-Telegram*. Rohe reported for newspapers such as the *Lawrence Journal*, the *Kansas City Star*, the New York *Evening World*, and the *Rocky Mountain News*. While in treatment for tuberculosis, she supported herself with freelance writing.

As the first female bureau chief of a major U.S. press service (United Press), she reported on the January 1915 earthquake that killed 32,600 people in Avezzano, Italy, and on World War I out of Rome; she also worked for the Red Cross. She interviewed Mussolini several times and conducted Sarah Bernhardt's last interview before her death. Unable to sustain a journalism career because she was not receiving pay equivalent to that of male correspondents, she eventually ceased writing to pursue an interest in Etruscan art.

"The Villa of Miracles"
From "Italy Keeps Its Troubles Secret"
Urbana [IL] *Daily Courier* 13 Aug. 1915: 3

Rome, July 14. (by mail.)—Six hundred wounded soldiers, the first visual horror of Italy's entrance into the war, arrived in Rome today.

Rome, emotional, responsive, gazed upon the unloading of the two train loads and their despatch in tram cars, ambulances and automobiles to the various hospitals. It was a sight long to be remembered. Traffic was stopped as the vehicles bearing the Red Cross passed through the city.

Women wept and men, hats in hand, cheered the returning wounded, while from the same depot fresh recruits were departing for the front.

So far Rome had gazed only upon these departing soldiers, banners had flown, and flowers had pelted the "soldati." Today all is changed. The little crown prince and his sisters, his mother, Queen Helena, and the Queen Mother Marguerite have been at the station to cheer the soldiers on their way to the mountains to join the men with the king [Victor Emmanuel III].

Today in the midst of the surging Roman crowd the crown prince again was among the people. Two wounded men in particular attracted his attention for they wore upon their breasts medals for bravery. Strongly affected at the sight of these two heroes the little prince insisted that they enter his automobile and be conducted to the hospital in his company. The Roman crowd watching the scene broke into cheers and wild demonstrations.

"Vive Prince Humbert!" "Vive Savoia!" "Vive the army!"

But the prince of Piedmont, future king of Italy, his eyes fastened eagerly on the two soldiers, began to question them eagerly.

"Have you seen papa—the king?"

The two soldiers, eyes filled with tears, voices broken with emotion, tried in vain to reply.

"I would like to go to the front and fight with the soldiers for Italy with papa," he said affectionately, trying, with childish sympathy, to encourage the two soldiers to talk.

"But have you seen papa?" he reiterated.

The two soldiers, weeping and laughing with emotion, replied:

"Yes, we have seen him. He gave us these medals with his own hands. He shook hands with us. He called us his brave sons."

"And how is he?" cried the crown prince.

"Fine," replied the soldiers, "and lighthearted when among us. He acts as though it were a holiday instead of a war."

Then the two soldiers recounted to the little prince all the details of the encounter in which they were injured. And not until he had seen them safely placed in the hospital would he leave their sides.

The number of wounded is being kept a secret throughout Italy. The Roman papers have not even been allowed to print the number of today's returning wounded.

From "Healing Mutilated Italian Soldiers by the Power of Suggestion"
Norwich [CT] *Bulletin* 3 Oct 1917: 12

"All fear abandon, ye who enter here!"

These are the invisible words, suspended beside the Italian tricolor, over the gateway of an American villa at Rome.

It is the Villa Wurts [aka Villa Sciarra], beauty spot on the Janiculum, and within its flower-rilled grottoes and shady walks the blind are made to see, the lame to walk, the mute to speak. It is the garden of hope, the oasis where the human will is supreme, the haven where wreckage of war, men cast into the waste of life, are saved from the refuse.

When men pronounced blind open grateful eyes it is upon a paradise of tranquil beauty, such as to wipe out forever the scars of war. Here is a vision to renew hope as they look through flowering avenues toward the great panorama of Rome stretched at their feet against a background of green Campagna and distant purple mountain.

• • •

In this lovely spot the generosity of George Wurts of Philadelphia has made it possible for one of Italy's most valuable and interesting cures to be effected.

The miracles performed are not by anesthetic and skilled surgeon's knife. The American villa, given with a "starting fund" by George Wurts to the Italian government as a hospital, is the Nevrocomic Militare, scientific institute, where psycho-therapeutics demonstrates the reality of miracles. Here the "false blind," the "false mute," who, having been given the ordinary cure for physical wounds, had been passed on to the inevitable human wreckage of war, are being rescued through the power of suggestion.

The results which the director, Dr. Giovanni Fabrizi, famous alienist and psichiatra [sic], has attained a complete cure of two-thirds of the mutilated who have passed beneath his skilled eye since Mr. Wurts turned over his villa for this work five months ago. Italy already has 30,000 of this "mutilatti," men who should come under the psycho-therapeutic cure. The Villa Wurts has accommodations for eighty and Dr. Fabrizi is working with unflagging devotion to save all the big number from the fate of going through life physically disabled, when the real trouble is merely functional nervous disturbance. It is a rescue work of double value to the soldiers and to the Patria, to separate these victims of nervous disorders from those organically crippled.

There were fifty of these interesting cases called from the cool workrooms, where they were making toys, to pass before us, showing their respective wounds and progress of recovery. They were in all varying degrees of cure or helplessness, those from whose struggling lips and throat came no sound and those who, with only an occasional hesitancy, told the stories of their gratitude to Dr. Fabrizi. There were those who, on crutches, dragged seemingly useless limbs and those who came proudly forward, crutches thrown aside, stalking like tiny children, glorying in their newly found motor accomplishment. There were those whose limp arms, showing bullet wounds, were but lifeless lumps of flesh, others who, responding to Dr. Fabrizi's suggestion, raised supposedly useless arms to their foreheads in military salute.

"Stop trembling!" cried Dr. Fabrizi, as an unfortunate, shaking as with the palsy, took his turn in the line of inspection. The man whose ever-moving arm showed a bullet-wound, continued to twitch and shake. Only by keeping his hand in his coat over his chest was the violent trembling less distressing.

"I tell you to stop trembling, you know you can, there's nothing the matter with your arm."

The man whimpered as the doctor seized the offending member and held it firmly.

"Now you see you don't have to tremble," he cried, looking into the soldier's eyes. "See, you are all right now. And don't put your hand back in your coat; let it hang free."

• • •

"There is nothing organically wrong with his arm," said Dr. Fabrizi. "Indeed, the first thing we ascertain when the wounded are brought here is to see if the trouble is organic or functional. If organic we turn the men over to other hospitals."

The man in question had been found wounded by shrapnel after several hours' exposure. He had been given first aid at the field hospital and then sent on to another hospital for the care of the physically wounded. He had been given the accepted treatment and had been passed on as an inevitably disabled product of the war.

"This next one," continued the doctor, "is a 'false blind.'" As he called out the name, "Lizzi," a handsome boy of twenty-two with soft brown eyes shaded by thick lashes, came forward, feeling his way with a cane.

"How many fingers before you?" asked the doctor.

"Five," replied the boy.

"And now?"

"Two." Right again.

"For nearly a year I could see nothing," he told me. "After I had been here a week Dr. Fabrizi made me discern light and shade—then objects—now— well, you just don't know what it means to a fellow who has been condemned to blindness to see again. He's making me see. Yes, it was gas that did it. When the projectile exploded I was blinded. I shut my eyes—"

"And he kept them closed six months," said Dr. Fabrizi. "Until he underwent the examination here it was supposed he was really blind, but there is nothing whatever the matter with the optic nerve. He merely has the will to see now. He takes the usual psycho-therapeutic treatment and he will be completely cured."

A gentle-visaged man with suffering marked upon his face came forward. He seemed about forty-five, but when I asked he told me he was only twenty-eight.

• • •

"For fifteen months I could not speak a word and now"—his eyes filled with the frank tears of a grateful Latin—"thanks to the wonder Dr. Fabrizi has brought into my life, my little children once more can hear their father's voice."

"Tell me what you experienced when you discovered you could not speak," I suggested.

"A bomb exploded. I was buried beneath dirt and debris. I was there perhaps three hours when I regained consciousness. Then I realized what had happened. I could hear our men moving about. I tried to call out to them. I knew they were stretcher bearers. I called, but no sound came. I couldn't understand, then I screamed—nothing—nothing! It was horrible to know they were so near and not be able to make them hear. Then once more I lost consciousness. The next I knew I was in the field hospital. And then, after fifteen months' silence, I was given my voice again."

The man suddenly caught the hand of Dr. Fabrizi and kissed it, trembling with emotion.

"There, there," said the doctor, "run along back to your work."

But it was plain to see that the gratitude of these simple soldiers who had fought and suffered for the Patria was more to him than the praise and remuneration of wealthier patients. Dr. Fabrizi, now capitano-medico in the service of his country, is one of Italy's alienists, famed in celebrated criminal cases.

It was his expert opinion that saved [Filippo] Cifariello, the sculptor, from paying the penalty for wife murder. At the outbreak of the war Dr. Fabrizi gave his services to Italy. It was Gen. [Luigi] Cadorna who, realizing the greater need of his skill in saving the nervous victims of the war, insisted that his place was not in the field hospitals. On a recent visit to Rome the commander-in-chief of Italy's army visited the institute in the Villa Wurts, and to Dr. Fabrizi's suggestion that perhaps he could serve better at the front he gave a definite refusal.

"You are fighting one of our big battles here on the Janiculum. My soldiers can't spare you."

And as they came forward these soldiers proved how they could not spare him.

• • •

A wiry little Sicilian, whose hands had been frozen in the Adamello, proudly picked up a pencil and put it in his pocket to show his new power. A one-time debonair Neapolitan, whose jauntiness had for months given way to melancholy brooding over his affliction, bared a wounded arm, condemned as useless, which was now working with returning power. A nerve-shattered little man, enunciating painfully, asked me if I had heard his friend, Fausto, who had re-learned to use his voice here in the Villa Wurts, sing at the big benefit at the Constanzi.

All tried to do their best as they stood before their beloved doctor. The mutes offered perhaps the most vivid demonstration of suggestion's power, especially the newcomers. When finally a sound came from their bravely struggling throats the joy and gratitude which shone in eyes that sought the doctor's was something that brought a mist to one's own.

"A sort of Lourdes here on the Janiculum—same principle," said the doctor, as the blind saw, the mute spoke and the lame walked.

"If you will step into this room you will see that we have a splendid equipment with radioscopic apparatus, electric diagnosis, electric therapeutics, vibro therapeutics, physical cure, but above everything else psycho-therapeutics."

The doctor led the way through an office where two medical lieutenants and a secretary were busily tabulating the data of each particular case, invaluable documents in the field of science. Through dining room and spotless dormitories, through supply departments furnished generously by the American Red Cross, we passed again into the workrooms.

"Occupation, congenial employment—that is one of the special points in curing these nervous cases," said the director.

Over the worktables bright-colored toys were coming into being, the faces of the workmen lighting up with pleasure as goose girls drove their wards over green fields and brave bersaglieri [marksmen] made their charge on Austrian foe. Some designed, others carved, some painted, and the finished products were the new art toys such as delight the childish heart.

"Naturally this is not a competitive factory—just an occupational cure for these soldiers," explained Dr. Fabrizi. "The boys have two hours here in the morning and two again in the afternoon—not enough to tire them. Their days are well planned for treatment, work and recreation—all three equally important parts of the cure."

We walked through cypress alleys, where haughty peacocks spread their gorgeous plumage, past a swan-decorated lake, toward the gateway of the American villa. Before us lay history-haunted Rome, glowing in the gold of approaching sunset, as with the glories of the past.

"All the glories of Rome are not of the past," I thought as I looked back at Dr. Fabrizi, bowing farewell from the gateway of the villa of miracles.

Item from the Washington Times, *22 Nov. 1915; note Rohe's presence in a feature titled "Men Who Write War News for the Times."*

Eliza Ruhamah Scidmore (1856–1928)

Born in Madison, WI, Eliza Ruhamah Scidmore graduated from Oberlin College in 1878 (although she seems to have been using the first name of Lillie at the time). Her brother, George Hawthorne Scidmore, was a diplomat, and she often traveled with him to his postings.

As a journalist, she published well-received articles as a correspondent for the *Chicago Tribune* and periodicals such as the *Century*. Her books focused on areas such as Japan, China, and Alaska. Scidmore was the impetus behind a major tourist attraction in Washington, DC. She had seen cherry trees in Japan in 1884 and believed they could enhance Washington's newly created West and East Potomac Parks. Snubbed by park and DC administrators, she wrote to First Lady Helen Taft and found a sympathetic audience. In March 1912, Taft and Iwa Chinda, wife of the Japanese ambassador, planted the first cherry trees at the Tidal Basin.

Scidmore became the first female board member of the National Geographic Society and served as an associate editor of its magazine. Among her articles for the magazine was her reporting on the June 1896 earthquake that hit Japan. She was in Japan at the time of that country's declaration of war against Germany in 1914. In fall 1918, she became a yeoman (F)—the Navy's designation of its wartime female recruits—with the paymaster general's office in Washington, DC. She later studied the League of Nations in Geneva.

"White Can Become Something Ranker than Yellow"
From "Japan's Platonic War with Germany"
The Outlook 23 Dec. 1914: 914–20

Japan joined very slowly and deliberately, evidently reluctantly, in the great war last summer; responded, as bound by her alliance to do whenever requested, and this time "to protect British commerce in the Eastern seas." So quietly and so slowly did the wheels of Government move towards that end that many hoped until the very last moment that Japan would not be embroiled at all. It meant a setback to all political plans and the breaking of the promise to reduce taxation by which Count Okuma [Shigenobu]'s party had come to power, in opposition to the military clique which had ruled so long unhindered and continually demanded more millions for more armament. The 16,000,000 yen surplus in the Treasury, which gave opportunity to reduce the business tax under which the mercantile classes were groaning, vanished into the 60,000,000 yen appropriated for the Shantung expedition, and the merchants stoically accepted the situation.

Throughout the whole affair Japan has been calm, quiet, self-contained—a splendid object-lesson of how to go to war and not lose your head. There was no boasting, no hurrahing, no noisy "On to Tsingtau!" The troops moved unseen, the expedition embarking from southern ports, and northern troops moving down by night trains to replace the departed garrisons in Kiushiu Castle towns. All the rules of war on land and sea, all the Hague conventions, and all the etiquette of slaughter on land, in the air, on and under the sea, have been scrupulously observed—a war with velvet gloves—"our platonic war" with Germany, as T[sunejiro]. Miyaoka has so cleverly described it.

Early on the morning of the 15th of August a few mounted lancers, preceding the Court carriages, escorted the Emperor and Empress and their suites to the railway station. All Nikko, upper and lower village people, officials and priests, and a thousand picturesque white-clad pilgrims on their way to the midnight ceremonies on the summit of Nantaisan, lined the streets in devout silence as the little cavalcade went by in the earliest sunrise. There was a council at the Tokyo palace that afternoon, and the ultimatum went to Germany, despatched through Italy, Switzerland, Holland, Denmark, Siberia, and America, to make sure that it reached Berlin promptly.

Not often in history has the whirligig of time brought about so picturesque an incident as that of Japan now in alliance with two of the Powers (France and Russia) that made the protest against Japan's retaining dearly won Port Arthur in 1905, "advising" the third Power (Germany) to withdraw from the Chinese mainland "for the sake of the peace of the Far East." It could not be called a rude or insulting note, for Japan employed the exact words and phrases of "advice" given her ten years ago, repeating the German note of 1905 verbatim. At the end of the China War in 1895 Japan could not match the great fleet of Russian, French, and German cruisers gathered at Chefu, all cleared for action to enforce their advice. Japan choked her pride and her wrath and submitted.

Resistance would have been folly; useless bloodshed the immediate result, and the further consequences incalculable.

Disregarding the Austrian example in ultimatums, Japan allowed Germany a week to return an answer to her advice, and a month for disarmament and withdrawal should Germany accept the advice. Upon receipt of the ultimatum in Berlin every Japanese in Germany was clapped into prison, the German Government explaining that it could not otherwise protect them. Japanese Embassy officers could not see or communicate with them, nor get the list of their names. One hundred and seventy-eight Japanese professors and students, valets, acrobats, shopkeepers, and even children, were so detained, with no definite charge against any one of them. Next the German Government seized £250,000 of Japanese Government money deposited in the Deutsche Bank in Berlin, and grim war was on without any answer being returned to the ultimatum.

Neither the ultimatum nor the declaration of war made any difference whatever in the condition of the German residents in Japan. No disturbance or demonstration was made, no change occurred in their relations or conditions. German reservists continued to leave for America and Tsingtau—even by Japanese vessels—and no one was arrested or molested.

With appreciation of what had befallen British, Russian, and French Ambassadors and Consuls as they left Berlin and other German cities, the German Ambassador in Tokyo was in a panic from the first week of August. His fears were so conspicuous and so unnecessary that the manifestation of them gave the one touch of gayety to the affairs of all nations that seethed in Tokyo's terrific heat. Count [Arthur von] Rex, elderly, stout, rheumatic, had suffered one strain to his nerves the winter that the bubonic plague threatened him at his post in Peking, and his alarms in Tokyo caused a further and more elaborate locking of gates and doors and shuttering of all the visible windows in his Embassy compound. Attachés living in other parts of Tokyo removed to the Embassy inclosure at once by his order. But even after the ultimatum expired and a state of war existed between Germany and Japan Count Rex and his staff lived on for a week in Tokyo and no demonstrations were made in the hot, deserted stretches of Nagatocho, where the lonely police and gendarmes watched one another day in and out.

The German Ambassador and his staff and his Consuls sailed August 30, and the remaining German community saw their officials off, with all the flowers and toasts, *"Hocks!"* and *"Auf Wiedersehens!"* their hearts desired, on the American steamer Minnesota for Seattle. One German yachtsman even cruised about the harbor in a catboat with the German flag at the mast bellowing his last regards by megaphone. The officers of the Japanese torpedo-boats, acting as guard ships for Yokohama, only smiled at this naive disregard of international etiquette. No imagination could picture a Japanese flag as assisting at a similar function in Hamburg's or Bremen's harbor with German torpedo-boats smiling on the scene.

Simultaneously with the declaration of war the Minister of Home Affairs, alarmed by the savage ways of war in Christian Europe, issued instructions concerning the protection of German subjects in Japan, securing them the same protection of person, property, and honor as before if they conducted themselves without prejudice to the interests of Japan and her allies. The Minister of Education warned teachers not to make imprudent remarks that might rouse the animosity of young students, and urged them to show every kindness and facility to German teachers and students who might be called to the colors. The Chief of Police in Tokyo reminded people that, although the two Governments "had entered into hostilities for good reasons," the people of the two countries as individuals should not act against each other in any way, and that the citizens of Tokyo should be more magnanimous than ever to those Germans who chose to remain; that they should not hold public meetings to inspire animosity, but always to be worthy members of a civilized country. Wherefore German residents went about their affairs as freely as American or Spanish residents. Of twenty-four German teachers in Government employ only three left to join the colors at Tsingtau, over fifty German teachers remained in private employ, and no students or classes showed disrespect or turbulence. German mining engineers continued their duties at distant mountain villages among thousands of laborers, and even the German editor of a subsidized newspaper continued his criticisms of everything Japanese, his philippics against England, and [Alabama congressman Richmond] Hobson prophesies of war between Japan and America. After one warning by the police his journal was suppressed and he was ordered to leave. Angered Britons, when they had cooled, realized that it would have been better to imprison him "for protection," as he speedily went to Peking and assumed charge of an anti-Japanese newspaper, and began to make things hum in that distracted, politics-ridden capital.

Contrary to European example, German Government money deposited in Japan was not touched, and the Deutsche Bank in Yokohama continues unhindered in its management. No German property was injured, no German molested. No one's German governess, valet, or employee of any kind was interfered with or imprisoned. Germans naively wrote their names in the lists for tennis tournaments, unconscious of the fact that not a British woman or child would tread the same court with them.

While this went on in Japan, non-combatant Japanese were still detained in German prisons and the vigorous representations of the American Ambassador in Berlin [James Watson Gerard] were unavailing. In October the German authorities, through the American Government, intimated that the Japanese prisoners would be released provided the Japanese Government gave a similar guarantee for the safety of German residents in Japan! If that were guaranteed, the German government would "not only release the Japanese but even afford them all facilities for departure." On October 27, through the still more strenuous efforts of Ambassador Gerard, twenty-one Japanese were delivered to him and sent under Embassy escort to Zurich, Switzerland; but thirty-eight Japanese remained in German jails, some of them the children of Japanese residents in Germany.

The Germans, one and all, bitterly resented Japan's coming into the war game. They could not accept the same logic and plea of loyalty to an ally by which they explained Germany's stand by her ally, Austria. They recounted unceasingly all that Japan owed to Germany in military and medical training, modern science, and art and philosophy. Japan even owes the life of Japan's Emperor [Yoshihito] to Germany, they said, since as a delicate child he was cared for by a German physician. They proved so convincingly that everything was due to contact with German culture that for once Commodore [Matthew] Perry had a rest, and no American made himself heard with that perennial, age-worn claim of the American after-dinner speaker in Japan: "We did it all"—i.e., started Japan in the path of modern science and progress. Are "We" and

"Commodore Perry" always to be crammed down the Japanese throat at the Japanese banquet board by the touring American?

The German officials left, protesting the ingratitude of the world and Japan. "Why, this war was not to come off until next spring," whimpered one German official's incautious wife; "and then we were all to have been safely home in Germany before it began." A most illuminating break, which the British circulated with gusto.

The German officials were convinced that the German army would be in Paris by September 15, before their ships could reach Seattle; that the war would be over in a few months; and that they would all return quickly to their dwellings, which they left intact, servants on duty, gardens growing.

There was no war thirst in Japan, no lingering animosity or resentment at the advice of 1895 that had robbed them of Port Arthur, no race hatred or cry of "white peril" when war was declared. Intellectual Japan grieved deeply at the necessity; every army surgeon and university professor was saddened at being arrayed against honored teachers, and was cut to the quick by the violent expressions of German professors and officials. "Japan biting at Europe's heel," and "robbing" and "stealing Tsingtau," often raised peals of merriment.

The Eighteenth Army Division and other divisions in the southern island furnished the force of thirty thousand men, under the command of Lieutenant-General [Mitsuomi] Kamio, which constituted the Shantung expedition. General Bannardiston [actually Nathaniel Walter Barnardiston] with twelve hundred British, eight hundred Wales Borderers, and eight hundred Indian troops joined the land force, and British ships took part in the blockade, the whole fleet commanded by Admiral Kato [Kanji]. The whole Japanese navy was in commission, but only small cruisers, torpedo-boats, and destroyers were at Tsingtau. The battle-ships and swift cruisers were off scouting the South Sea for the marauding German cruisers, keeping the ways of commerce safe for merchant ships, concentrating with the British ships towards the South American coast, and escorting the great fleet of transports that bore the Australian contingent of 35,000 troops as far as Suez.

As the blockading fleet took position off Tsingtau, August 25, a typhoon swept the coast, and it was followed by a second and fiercer typhoon, that scattered the ships and made landing from transports a difficult affair at

Laitschou Bay, one hundred miles north of Tsingtau. Shantung Province was flooded as it has not been flooded in sixty years; rivers rose until whole valleys were inundated; villages of mud-walled houses melted into these lakes; and crops were drowned. The trenches around Tsingtau were filled or washed away, embankments crumbled, wire entanglements collapsed, and hidden land mines were exposed. All Shantung was a mud slough after the waters fell, and it was a fortnight before the last Japanese contingent and the heavy siege guns were landed. Through sloughs of mud they reached the shores of Kinochau Bay, and farther inland seized a station of the German railway line leading up three hundred miles to the provincial capital of Tsinanfu. This railway, connecting with the Tientsin-Pukow line from the Yangtze, which was German property and partly owned by the German Government, was seized for all its length, its bridges rebuilt, its coal mines relieved of their hidden explosives, and the locomotive fitted with missing parts. By this railway the Germans had received war materials, food supplies, reservists from all parts of China, and the returning crew of the disarmed Austrian cruiser which had been interned in earliest August. The Germans had been making belated efforts to transfer their railway to some neutral Power, but the neutral Legations at Peking were firm against any such entanglement. The British Minister seemed to be the only one in Peking whose advice Yuan Shi-kai asked for and followed, and when things were at more than boiling-point at Tsinanfu, and the German officials were threatening, Yuan Shi-kai sent them his trusted political adviser, Dr. [George Ernest] Morrison, formerly of the London "Times." To those familiar with the tangle of Peking's personal politics of the last decade this was another rare touch of humor in the gloomy world. Throughout the siege Tsingtau had had communication by wireless with both Peking and Shanghai, and the Chinese officials were well-nigh distracted by British and Japanese demands that this means of communication cease.

From the very first the Japanese announced that it would be a slow campaign, their first object being to avoid all possible loss of life on either side. It was their hope that the besieged would see the folly of prolonging operations and surrender while they could make terms.

But the Kaiser exhorted the garrison at Tsingtau to hold out to the end, as he would rather see the enemy in Berlin than lose his empire in the east. The Japanese called for surrender, and the Governor, Meyer Waldeck, answered:

Never shall we surrender the smallest bit of ground over which the German flag is flying. From this place we shall not retreat. If the enemy wants Tsingtau, he must come and take it.

It was reported that there was a strong feeling for surrender on the part of the three thousand German reservists, under the age of forty-five, drawn from business and professional life in all parts of the Far East. No reinforcements nor outside aid could ever be expected, and it was only a tedious wait for certain death, the practical ones said. The Governor and the military officers would not listen to talk of surrender, and duels were fought over the suggestion. From time to time reservists who had no stomach for fighting against such forlorn hope, or who reasoned that live Germans in Hankow or Shanghai were better than dead one in Tsingtau, slipped away by night, reappeared in those cities, and unblushingly defended their conduct. Several reservists even returned to Japan while the siege went on, and one German officer, Major Derkenman, military adviser to Yuan Shi-kai, who had left that billet to go to Tsingtau in early August, returned to Peking and resumed attendance on Yuan Shi-kai. It was farcical after that to insist upon the Chinese interning the crew of the German torpedo-boat stranded on a rock as they were effecting their escape from beleaguered Tsingtau. It was boldly suggested in print that Japanese aviators should distribute maps showing a convenient back door left open every night for such reservists as wished to abandon Tsingtau before it was too late.

Before the general attack on the posts began, October 22, the Japanese called a second time for surrender and gave opportunity for the non-combatants to leave. The American Consul, some women and children, and priests were passed from one boat to another in a rough sea outside the harbor, where more than a thousand fixed and floating mines had been dredged up and snared. Chinese junks past counting had been blown up, as well as one Japanese cruiser and destroyers of both sides, by these mines. A band of women shell-divers from the province of Ise offered their services to clear away the mines, but the Japanese authorities denied them emphatically. They were puzzled and aghast at foreigners' applause and approval of such an impossible thing as women taking any part in military work. Some kink in the Japanese brain made the thing so absurd and improper that no Japanese whom I knew could agree with me that it was the most picturesque incident of the war. Any one who has seen those Ise women somersault down into Toba Bay and crawl around for three and five whole minutes before coming up with a pearl shell knows that they could have dealt with fixed and floating mines as easily.

The real bombardment of the inner forts began on October 31, the Emperor's official birthday, "as prearranged," they might have said; for a party of high officials, foreign military *attachés*, and members of Parliament had been waiting for a fortnight in Tokyo ready to embark on a despatch boat to Tsingtau "to watch operations in Shantung."

The first lot of prisoners, seventy-seven in all, and all captured on outpost duty, were brought to Japan early in October and assigned to Kurume, on the southern island, the headquarters of the Eighteenth Army Division. They were received at the station with ceremony by the military officers of the garrisons, by Mrs. Kamio and the members of the local Red Cross Society. I visited them myself later. The men were quartered in a Buddhist preaching-hall and classrooms, the officers in the Lord Abbot's rooms at the Bairingi Temple, and the wounded men in a separate ward of the military hospital, where the chief surgeon and all his attendants spoke German. Officers, men, and invalids were allowed to speak to me freely, and one and all acknowledged the courtesy, consideration, and unfailing kindness of the Japanese officers in charge. As with the Russian prisoners of war in 1904 and 1905, the Japanese are doing "As the Hague Ordains" [a reference to a book by Scidmore] and then doing even a little more for their charges.

The captives are kept at different old castle towns, now headquarters of military divisions in the southern islands, in order to gain the advantage of mild winter weather. Buddhist temples and preaching-halls have been rented for such use, and are readily adapted to the purpose. The prisoners live under the most lenient regulations, and the Prisoners' Information Bureau in Tokyo permits communication, takes charge of any consignments, and answers any letters of inquiry concerning the captives. The prisoners' families may join them, rent houses in the towns, and the prisoners may live there with them under light restrictions, as Russian prisoners were permitted to do in 1904 and 1905.

I once heard a blustery American take a Japanese to task for exhibiting at the Panama Exhibition. "Why do you help make this fair a success in the State and the city where Legislature, press, and people have so abused you? Pay them back, draw out, save your money!" thundered the irate one. "They'll never thank you."

"Ah," was the answer, "that would be a very small spirit, to show resentment in such way. Japan rejoices more than other nations that the Panama Canal is complete. We can make a first exhibit of Japanese magnanimity, perhaps."

Since the war began Japan has been courted by all the Powers in Europe and directed and indirectly appealed to for help. In season and out, M. [Stéphan] Pichon, former Minister of Foreign Affairs, has argued in print for a Japanese contingent in Europe; he remembers and always acknowledges generously that he, while French Minister at Peking, owed his life, as did all the other foreigners, to the stiff defense of the Su Wang Fu by Colonel Shiba [Gorō] and his Japanese guards and volunteers. Besides troops—a whole army corps, it is said, the Russians have called for to strike the sure terror to the heart of the enemy which they themselves experienced when Nogi [Maresuke]'s men from Port Arthur fell upon the Russian right at Mukden—besides a fighting contingent, there has been a call for a body of one hundred thousand Japanese coolies to intrench, that feature of the division of military labor having impressed all foreign observers of the war in Manchuria.

It is comforting to any people to be appreciated, to have their merits and abilities acknowledged, to be the honored ally of Great Britain, and to work with her in military and naval undertakings; but Japan has not at all lost her head with all the successes, courting, and coaxing and flattery that have gone on. She knows she is a great Power, with a great navy, and an army second to none in merciless efficiency and first in humanity and chivalry, and her people have no notion of mixing in the European mess, of marching to the shambles of Europe, of dying for any other emperor than their own. Despite Congressman Hobson's warnings and prophesies and the machinations of the Peking press and diplomatic wire-pullers and of the American masquerader in Tokyo [possibly a reference to J. Ingram Bryan, a professor in Tokyo], she does not want to and is not "going to war" with America. It would not pay, and Japan is a very hard-headed, practical Japan since the last war left her the great legacy of taxes. Japan is not striving to gain "the supremacy of the Pacific"—if that means ninety per cent of the commerce and carrying trade—because she already has it, and has had it without realizing that it was anything to make a great fuss about. Four merchant ships under the American flag are a pitiful plea for "supremacy;" and, more than this, our strangling navigation laws, the tyranny of labor unions, and the solidarity of the labor vote will forever check the United States from getting any more of the supremacy. As good neighbors and mutual customers, the one needing silk and tea as much as the other needs raw cotton and machinery and wheat, there is room and chance for both without jealousy and crowding and blocking.

If ever there was the retort courteous, just retribution, and also an object-lesson that no country can ignore, the Japanese have afforded it in this little war at Tsingtau, a campaign that they entered upon with deliberation and dignity, with every courtesy and honor to the enemy, without boasts or threats, gibes or jeers at their opponents, and without any interference whatever with non-combatants. The whole campaign was conducted according to the rules of war and of chivalry. "*Noblesse oblige*" is easily translated into "the way of the Samurai," and *bushido*, in working even in the field, should be contrast give acute heart-searchings and violent blushes to some in Europe.

There was never any ranting in print, never recourse to petty retaliation, no descent into mediaeval savagery. It was a duty, and it was performed with thoroughness and efficiency. Japan has been a loyal ally, an honorable foe, and incidentally has set an example to Christian Europe and shoveled hot coals on Australia's head until the antipodes ought to sizzle. She has turned the other cheek to white Australia, and turned the tables with a magnanimity they must acknowledge. Let us hope that we have done with those senseless catch-words, "the Yellow Peril." This very war has raised too many embarrassing questions as to what is white and which is yellow, and shown that white can become something ranker than yellow, and that Christians may get a lesson in Christian-like conduct from those whom they have essayed to teach.

It was necessary to destroy the Germans' stronghold on the Asiatic mainland and their coaling and wireless stations throughout the South Seas in order to protect commerce and trade and industry. Japan must have wool from

Australia and cotton from America and iron from China to keep her factories running, and silk and tea and small wares must go to America if Japan's people are to live and pay taxes. Her commerce must be protected at all cost, and, thanks to her navy, Japanese steamships have crossed the Pacific back and forth unhindered, keeping to their fixed schedules just as they did last year.

There have been gay little by-plays in the Pacific to relieve the hideous tales of the war in Europe. "The Marshall Islands must be taken. There's coal and a wireless station there," said the British Admiralty lords. The Japanese went— only eight hundred miles, two days' steaming from Japanese island shores—and took them, and handed them over to Australia with an indifferent, "You may have them if you want them," that ought to rest America's hair-trigger nerves. The capture of the Marshall Islands was a gay little comedy that should get into comic opera yet. There was no fighting, no shot fired in anger, no defense by the little body of Germans at Jaluit when the Japanese cruisers came. Two surveying schooners sank themselves into the bay, an imprisoned Japanese copra buyer was set free, and the German Governor given two hours to get ready to go to Japan on the man-of-war. At Yokosuka, the naval station in Yeddo Bay, the German Governor of Jaluit and his family were put on a torpedo-boat and rushed up to Yokohama at a gait of thirty miles an hour—to a Japanese dungeon and chains, of course, the gloomy Germans thought. A charming young American Vice-Consul, in a high hat and frock coat, and the chairman of the German residents' committee, also in gala array, were waiting to receive the Jaluit party at the *hatoba* [wharf]. The Japanese officers in charge presented his passengers, clicked his heels together, saluted, and was gone— racing back to Yokosuka at full speed. "Where am I to go?" wailed the Governor of Jaluit, and the two high hats conveyed him in a shining motor car to the Grand Hotel. "*Where* am I to go? Where *am* I to go?" he insisted, demanding to know his prison place. It was long before he could comprehend that he might go wherever he pleased, that the Japanese Government wanted none of him, was done with him, and would be only too pleased to have him go soon. German funds were forthcoming from the Deutsche Bank, and he betook himself to Honolulu, where there is a powerful German community and a new German colony of the interned Geier's crew and the crews of German merchant ships that wait the end of the war with him.

Tsingtau was small game, a by-play only of this great war to the victors of Port Arthur, Mukden, and Tsushima. The manner and the good manners of that capture—which they graciously let stand as a surrender, since the white flags rose only as the storming parties rushed through the last breach—their courtesy to the vanquished, their kindness to the prisoners, are the greatest glory of the exploit.

Japan has said that she will ultimately return Tsingtau to China, administering it until the Peace Conference permits her to negotiate with China. A peaceful and prosperous Shantung, growing beans and silk to ship by the Japanese railway and Japanese ships from the free port of Tsingtau, will pay her best in the long run, and Japan would gain nothing by holding on to Tsingtau. All Europe grinned and scoffed when we said that we would return Cuba after the Spanish[-American] War, but we did retire, and occupied and retired from it even a second time. If the meddlers in Peking will only cease to stir strife, China can date a great prosperity from the return of Tsingtau to its owner, never again to be alienated to any European Power. In the last months the Germans wrecked all the public buildings, the docks and wharves, and shell fire destroyed the great barracks and forts, the water-works, and the electric light works. The young forests were cut away on the land side to give the guns sweep, the forty miles of perfect automobile roads were neglected, and forty million marks of German taxpayers' tribute have gone for naught. German trade and commerce are paralyzed, perhaps never to recover, and German merchants, once on the pinnacle of prosperity, are ruined throughout the East.

"Imperturbable Sangfroid"

From the citation for the Croix de Guerre for Florence Church Bullard of the American Ambulance Corps, qtd. in *The Woman Citizen* 10 May 1919: 1079.

Ruth Stanley Farnam (de Luze) (1873–1956)

Ruth Stanley Farnam, passport photo, n.d. From A Nation at Bay *(1918), facing p. 12.*

Born in Patchogue, NY, Ruth Stanley married Yale graduate Charles H. Farnam Jr. in 1899, and they lived in Rownhams House in Southampton, England. Her husband died in 1909. During the war she served in Serbia with Princess Alexis Karageorgevitch (aka American Myra Pratt) during a typhus epidemic and later with Mabel Dunlop Grouitch, the American wife of Serbian minister Slavo Grouitch who had organized a hospital in Belgrade. Farnam's duties ranged from supervising medical and relief supplies to working as a surgical nurse, and she traveled to the front. Given the honorary rank of sergeant in the Serbian army, she raised substantial funds for Serbian relief. In Greece, she attended to refugee matters. Farnam was decorated by the Serbian and Greek governments. In February 1928 she married Baron Raymond de Luze, head of the French winery Maison Ackerman.

"My Education in the Grimness of War"

From *A Nation at Bay: What an American Woman Saw and Did in Suffering Serbia* (1918): 174–92

At this time the Serbians, French and English had succeeded in driving the enemy back as far as place called Bröd on a very recent offensive. Here both sides had "dug in." The Serbian lines were just outside Bröd, while the enemy lines ran through the streets of this Serbian town. Thither we directed our course the day following my official permission.

The afternoon of my last day at the hospital was spent in climbing the hills around the hospital whence we could get glimpses of the town of Ostrovo and of the road leading away to the Front. Occasionally an ambulance would crawl out of the far hills and come down the winding road to the hospital. Now and again an aeroplane would float into view and circle about, reflected in the glassy mirror of the Lake of Ostrovo—and then suddenly dart away in the direction of Florina.

. . . .Along the shores of the beautiful lake, with its tiny islands bathed in the rosy light of just-before-sunrise, through a valley of deep clogging sand and then a long ascent into the rocky hills over which our gallant Ford struggled and coughed and rattled and tugged. Sometimes we would have to wait, turned sidewise on some almost precipitous slope while the engine gathered itself together for some supreme effort to get us to the top. Once there, we slid and bounded and almost tumbled down over big stones and holes, only to begin another toilsome climb worse than the last.

We overtook and passed the French troops of . . . yesterday's outing, but now they were seated by the roadside, having their morning meal, and they waved their steel helmets and cheered as we joggled by.

At the edge of a level plain the road branched away to the left to the French base at Florina, but we kept to the right until the road curved into a little ruined village—Old Vrbéni. From the moment we took the road at the fork the flat country had shown signs of the heavy fighting which had so recently taken place over this territory.

Everywhere were rolls of cruel barbed-wire, neatly stacked shell cases and the baskets in which they are handled, broken rifles, scraps of metal and all the various debris of battle. The earth looked like rudely plowed land, so pitted and torn with shell holes was it, and everywhere were the rude earthworks which had been thrown up by Serb and Bulgar. Sometimes these were a long line of mud embankments behind which many men could shelter; but more often the earth was scooped out in a tiny nest like a hare's "form." Some of these faced North and some South. There were many into which the earth had been roughly shoveled back and we knew that these held Bulgarian dead.

The Serbians were buried in plots of ground carefully marked off by rows of field stones; over the graves were small wooden crosses, new and shining—yellow like gold. When we passed one of these, my companions crossed themselves and I think we all offered up a silent prayer for brave men living who are fighting for all that is true and just on earth, for liberty and peace; and for brave men dead, who had fallen for these glorious ideals.

Our car was turned through a gap in the hedge and we rolled into a level field. Before us we saw a tent into which stretchers holding motionless forms were being carried. This was the dressing station nearest to the Serbian line. Within the tent soldiers with their wounds dressed lay upon the bare ground, at best with only a handful of straw under them and still in their ragged and soiled uniforms.

There were no ambulances up there and the wounded were brought in from the battlefield on stretchers carried by two men. We saw also a curious contrivance of two large wheels with a sort of stretcher hung from the axles. This could be managed by one man, though as it jolted over the stony ground the wounded man would groan in agony. Every time a man would cry out Colonel [Roman] Sondermayer [head of the Serbian Military Medical Service] would flinch and his eyes grow dark with pain. When he spoke to or examined men in the tents he was like a tender father. The soldiers adored him.

After half an hour we went on to an inn on the other side of the village, and here I was presented to the Commander-in-Chief of the Serbian Army, Voivode Mishitch. Not tall, rather lightly built, this wonderful soldier does not impress a stranger with a sense of power until one meets the full, direct look of his eyes. Then one sees that here is a *man*. Calm, impersonal, his look bores into one's inmost being, and I should not care to see him angry—*with me* at any rate.

He was much interested in hearing of my work and asked if I wanted to go yet nearer to the battle line. To my emphatic affirmative he said, "We will see what can be done," and after we had had coffee, Major Todorovitch, his aide-de-camp, was sent for, given his instructions, and we bade the Voivode "au revoir," climbed into our faithful car and started again toward the roaring guns.

Just outside the village stood a group of captive Bulgarians, whose guards saluted us, grinning with triumph as we passed. About a mile further on we saw eight hundred or more Bulgarian prisoners in their earth-brown uniforms standing in groups by the roadside or bathing their feet in the ditch. The Serbian guards were sharing their scanty store of tobacco with these men and, remembering the horrors of the Bulgarians' treatment of Serbian prisoners and wounded upon the battle-field, I could only wonder at their charity.

In the almost demolished villages we saw ragged, haggard women winnowing corn, tossing it in the air with weary gestures, while near them sat the pale emaciated children who had forgotten how to romp and play—whose only thought now seemed to be "when shall we get something to eat?". . . Further along the road a little girl lying on the low bank smiled at me, but her yellow skin drawn over the sharp bones told a tragic story. I stopped the car and went back to see if I could do anything, but when I spoke to her she did not answer. I took her in my arms but she was already dead. "What was the trouble?" I asked.

"She was my child. She had great hunger," the mother replied simply. I gave the mother some cakes of chocolate, which was all I had with me, and some money, but the low voiced "Fala" [thanks] of these wretched people was so hopeless that the tears ran down my face and I felt that my heart would break.

. . . .[I]n the blue sky I saw a flash of silver as the sun glinted on a wire or a wing. Behind it in the clear air grew suddenly three tiny, fleecy puffs of cloud— then three more—and three more. The plane must have been "burning the wind," as it was not visible to us for more than five minutes altogether, and we had seen it as soon as it lifted over the mountains before us. It was a Serbian machine and the lovely, soft cloudlets were the deadly, exploding shrapnel with which the enemy batteries were pursuing it.

Down the hillside came a string of mules, each laden with a sort of pack-saddle holding two rude chair-shaped structures and in one of these on either side sat a wounded man. Other wounded men began to meet us, some with roughly bound-up heads and with streaks of dried blood on their faces; some with arms in improvised slings and one boy who limped by with a bandage around one leg and blood dripping from it to the dust.

Where two stones rudely set in the earth marked a boundary, Major Todo-rovitch saluted.

"Madame," he said, "I have the honor to inform you that you are the first woman of any nationality to enter reconquered Serbian territory." All this time the thunder of guns had been growing louder and louder and at last we halted on a little plateau on which were a number of small tents and a line of fine cavalry chargers. Half a dozen officers, French and Serbian, came out to meet us and were surprised to see a woman—and above all, a *foreign* woman—there.

. . . . Under shelter of the rock they led me to the brink of a precipice and here I was able to stand between two great out-cropping leaves of stone, while I gazed at a battlefield spread in relief below. Level with the face of precipice, and of course far below my eyrie, were the Serbian trenches with the big guns some distance behind them and the village . . . some distance away on their left.

Every now and then a Bulgarian shell would fall among the little red-tiled houses and a cloud of dust and whirling leaves would rise, circle about and slowly settle. Once a riderless horse galloped out and then a stretcher was carried slowly away toward the dressing station—then another and another. From the mountains still further to the left, which run like a great spine from Florina to Monastir and sweep round beyond in a rocky curve, came the great shells from the French guns and the white and dun clouds of vapor from the explosions formed constantly drifting veils over the tortured valley.

. . . . Once I saw a group of men, perhaps eight of them, mashed to a gory pulp by three shells which fell close together in the Serbian line, and a man close by who had apparently been untouched, but suffered a temporary derangement due possibly to tortured nerves, sprang out of the trench and, shaking his fists in the direction of the enemy, rushed blindly forward toward the river, into which he plunged and was lost to view.

Still dazed and gasping, I heard Colonel Milovanovitch ask, "Would you like to give the signal for our guns to recommence firing?" and, shaking with emotion, I nodded assent.

So, in the name of American Womanhood, I gave the signal which sent shells roaring over the valley to fall in the Bulgarian trenches. And the men behind me shouted "Givela Amerika! [Give, America]."

I was shaking from head to foot . . . Major Todorovitch spoke—

"Calm yourself, Madame; they have not just got our range up here yet. When it grows *too* dangerous we will take you away."

"Do you think I am afraid?" I cried. "I never *lived* before!"

Edith Marjorie Hulsizer (Copher) (1891-1935)

Marjorie Hulsizer, ca. 1916. From the Microcosm, *Simmons College Annual, p. 62.*

Marjorie Hulsizer was born and raised in Flemington, NJ, where her lawyer father, Abraham Chalmers Hulsizer, served as mayor and postmaster, and was a prominent figure in the local Democratic Party. She graduated from Simmons College in 1916 with a degree in home economics and a reputation for *sang froid* (according to her college yearbook). One of the few U.S. female dietitians serving overseas during World War I, she worked in Base Hospital No. 5, the Harvard Unit headed by noted surgeon Harvey Cushing that was attached to the British Expeditionary Force and often subject to attack by the Germans. She served in Étaples and Boulogne-sur-Mer in France. In December 1918, she transferred to Base Hospital No. 57

of the American Expeditionary Force and remained there until fall 1919. The British and French governments decorated her for her service.

Hulsizer became the chief dietitian at Barnes Hospital in St. Louis and married surgeon Glover Hancock Copher ca. 1925. A daughter, Marjorie Anne, was born in 1930. After Hulsizer's death from cancer in 1935, an annual award of the Academy of Nutrition and Dietetics was established in her name to honor achievement in nutrition.

"A Great Big Circus, with a Great Many Little Side Shows"
"Miss Hulsizer Writes Another Interesting Letter from 'Somewhere in France'" *Hunterdon* [NJ] *Republican* 4 Jul. 1917: 1

General Hospital (U.S. Army Base Hospital No. 5),
British Expeditionary Force,
May 31, 1917

Dear Family:

We left London yesterday and came across to France. It took us two hours to cross the channel, I presume because of the heavy fog. We had some destroyers guarding us, which with the fog made us quite safe. We came to our present camp in big buses or vans that smelled of carbolic or sulphur-napthal very strongly. The sights outside of the van as we came along the country roads distracted our olfactory nerves, however. The first thing that impressed me before we left the docks was the passing of many soldiers. They were the men who had been home on leave—eight months' service, ten days' leave—and were returning to the front. They all carried their kits on their backs, clothes, rations, trench hats, guns or rifles, and some carried huge loaves of bread that were sticking out in interested fashion as if they too wanted to see the sights. Really, so many of them went by our windows that it seemed as if two of our U.S. armies must have gone by. I never in all my life saw so many soldiers. They all seemed to be in a cheerful mood; some of them grinned at us and ... saluted us or our colors.

. . . . There are about four or five hospitals bunched in together here. Each hospital has its wards, which are for the most part tents, some shacks; its nurses' quarters shacks or huts of from four to seven rooms, each room holding two nurses. Its officers' quarters, huts, I think, but I am not sure. Its enlisted men's quarters, its disinfecting power plant (one for all), and its canteen store. As you look down on the hospitals, all you can think of is a great big circus, with a great many little side shows. There are walks and gulleys all around the tents and shacks, and a good macadam road runs the length of the hospitals. There are some tennis courts for the nurses and doctors, and we are to have some bicycles for recreation. Very near us there are troops—machine gun corps being trained for the front. Over our heads aeroplanes sometimes fly. We can hear gun practice and rifle practice. There are troops, troops, troops everywhere. The railroad runs right by us, and we see troop trains go by with soldiers for the front. The front is between forty and fifty miles off, and at night, at times, I expect we will be able to hear the shelling.

. . . . This country is so fresh and beautiful one cannot comprehend that there is a war forty miles away, murdering people wholesale. Although our quarters are rough, and we are going to have to do and see a great many things that we have never done or seen before, I am gladder than I've been that I have come. It seems so terrible not to do anything, just to sit back and watch. I feel now as if I never could do or think a thoughtless act again. It grips you and gets you[,] this hellish war.

. . . . June 1, 1917. . . .You may be interested to know that my job is to run the nurse's [sic] mess and keep their quarters clean. The British unit has had a nurse to do this that they call the home nurse. Until I get a little adapted, it is going to be slow going. Marketing at present is my most difficult as well as most delightful task. I go in twice a week with a sergeant to help lift and carry things.

To-day I went with the Home Sisters (the chiefs of the old unit are staying in order to settle us in our new work and show us the ropes.) We went to two nearby towns the quaintest places I ever saw. The market place is in the center of the town and there curious old women come and bring their vegetables, flowers, fish, etc., to sell. Some of them have baskets, others have regular stalls. We go in among the crowd, look at the products, ask prices and buy as reasonably as we can. . . . . After finishing at the market square in this little town, we went on to another place and visited some real shops.

. . . .We heard firing while in the shop and of course rushed out of doors. People were in the streets watching shrapnel burst in the air above and the bursting shrapnel was for our enemy aeroplane sailing along. The gunners that I saw went wide of the mark. There was an English flying corps officer standing next to me and he said that the shrapnel didn't get anywhere near the plane and probably the people in it didn't even know they were being fired on. It seemed probable because they kept straight on in their course and did not try to dodge. Finally we lost sight of them as they went into the sun and the clouds about it. When we returned to camp we heard that the plane had been brought down. They say they get the scouting aeroplanes every time.

June 2, 1917. This morning I have fussed around and made sandwiches for tea this P.M. It is a whale of a chore. We have to use rolls and cut them in threes, then they are buttered, filled and cut across again four times. My mess cook is a very gentle lad from Mississippi. At present he doesn't know much cookery but frying. We are also having to help us what the English call P.B. men, i.e., permanent base men, who are not fit for active fighting, but can do the hospital sort of thing very decently.

...[A] little garden has been planted here for the nurse's mess by the Home Sister (she whose place I take) and we reap the benefit later. We have oceans of peas, cauliflower, cabbage, lettuce and potatoes. I have one more patch to plant to potatoes if I can get it done.

We have been given army cots and they are more comfy. We also have a swell little folding arm chair, a lantern, a canvas water bucket and a canvas basin. Yesterday our boys put up our beds for us and I wish you could have seen them hustle. It was done in a minute.

"The Hut Shook and So Did I."
Letter, Hulsizer Family Papers, Library of Congress, Manuscripts Division

Somewhere in France
September 15, 1917
Dearest Family:
. . . . You ask if I fell out of the Hut Door, Mother, when I sprained my ankle. There was a girl sitting on the door-step on a blanket. I tried to jump over her, caught my foot in the blanket, and fell on the ground outside.

Have you seen in the Papers that [Camp Hospital] No. 11 was bombed nearly two weeks ago? On Labor Day night we had a dance at the Hospital.

Glorious moonlight outside. In the midst of the dancing, the electric lights suddenly went out. Candles were assembled and we carried on, after drawing the curtians [sic, curtains] for precaution's sake. Lights out over here means hostile airplanes. There had been a big air-raid in Boulogne the night before. Several people being killed. None of us were nervous, only interested and excited. That night nothing happened. . . . Tuesday night there was a sort of rumor about a raid and I left word to be wakened if there was any excitement, as I usually sleep through all noise. . . . . At 11 o'clock I was awakened by Alice [Cunningham] calling to me, "Get up Hulsey, there go the guns." We both jumped out of bed and into slippers and coats—and then out of doors. We'd not much more than got out when there were two explosions. I thought in [it?] the anti-air craft guns, but it seemed to shake everything so that I ran to one of the huts and leaned against it. I'd just got there when very near there was a tremendous explosion. The hut shook and so did I. There were other explosions after that two in quick succession. Searchlights about five met at a point in the middle of the sky. The moon was absolutely ripping and the night quite calm. The nurses ran around the quarters very much excited. We none of us thought anything had happened until we heard that the operating room nurses had been sent for. Then some of the V.A.D. [British Voluntary Aid Detachment nurses] hurried into their clothes and went down to the Wards. I met two of them when they came back and dismayed to hear that bombs have been thrown, several people killed and many more injured. The next morning we discovered that a Hun raider had come over the Hills, dropped two bombs at [former British General Hospital] No. 18 (Chicago Unit, [known as Base Hospital No. 12]) but done no damage, crossed the camp street, dropped one in No. 4 (English), also harmless, then flew directly over our officer's [sic] quarters. Major [Roger I.] Lee and the C.O. stood talking in front of the C.O.'s tent. They had heard the first bombs and the C.O. had just remarked to Major Lee that he'd go over and cheer the nurses up, etc., when a bomb burst right in the officer's quarters, three or four tents back of the C.O. Lt. [William T.] Fitzsimmons, our new adjutant, was killed instantly. Three other M.O.'s were injured—none of them in the original Unit. Bombs were also dropped in the Wards and the Reception Tent (where patients were received from the ambulances). Three of our enlisted were killed and two patients. Several others were slightly wounded. One of the nurses, Miss [Eva Jean] Parmalee, was a regular brick. A bomb dropped in her Ward and nearly demolished one end. She was perfectly cool and kept her end up wonderfully. After the excitement died down a bit, she went to take a man's temperature, felt for her watch and found that it had been cut right off the leather strap from which it hung at her waist. Her apron had been cut above it and her coat riddled with holes. Evidently her watch saved her from death or a nasty wound. [Parmalee later received the Distinguished Service Cross for her actions during the raid.] That night after the raid Al[ice] and I pulled our beds together and made Judy sleep with us. I slept on the crack and put my legs in with Alice and the rest of me with Julie [sic]. We slept about two minutes consecutively the rest of the night. Since then we have had more scares and not without reason, but so far nothing has happened. The M[edical]. O[fficers].'s have been most kind and dug trenches for us. We had a scare last night after I came home from church and Alice and I tried our trench out. It was rather a close fit, but we stuck it till the light came on again. . . .

All the English have been so kind and considerate about the whole affair. To them raids mean nothing new. They've had so many. I expect they are more or less hardened. To say the least, it was a great shock to us. . . .

Will you be good enough to look about my books Mother, dear, and send me a series of twelve or fifteen lectures on Dietetics? I think they are type-written and all in a bunch. Later on I may have to give some lectures to the enlisted men and I should like a few notes to brush up on. Not using all that dope makes it lie in the distant fields of my mind shrouded with mist and quite inaccessible, I am afraid.

"A Huge Round Ball of Fire Dropping Through the Air"
Letter, Hulsizer Family Papers, Library of Congress, Manuscripts Division

May 26, 1918
Same old place
Dearest Family:

. . . . I do not wonder, Mother, that you were a bit alarmed about the Channel Ports. We all were more or less. I had my bag packed for a week ready to leave at a moment's notice. They said that twenty thousand civilians left B. [possibly Boulogne] inside of one week. The longer the offensive is delayed, the less likely they are to break through. Our defences are getting stronger every minute. Lloyd George seems to think that we are building subs faster than Germany can sink them. . . . . Captain Simeon told me that he thinks the war will be over by the Fall. . . . I am not as optimistic as that, but I do think they are cooked—although it may take a year or so to make them see it that way.

Did you see in the papers of the last atrocity of the Huns, bombing Hospitals? It happens to be the town that I went to Market in last summer and a little in the place where we are. The Huns in dropping the first bomb set fire to a soldiers' recreation Hut or Tent. The blaze made them think they had an Ammunition Dump and they circled round above that Hospital dropping about twenty bombs in the same place—nurses and M.O.'s were killed outright or so much wounded that they died ultimately—patients and orderlies and guards. ... There was a tremendous barrage put up here that same night. I heard the Hun's motor above us very distinctly, but the barrage was such a good one that he couldn't get through it. He tried about four or five times. I think I went downstairs five times and into the wine cellar. All I remember is getting out of bed, going into the wine cellar and vice versa so much that the last time I was so sleepy that I nearly fell over coming back up. The barrage lasted until nearly 1:30 p.m. Gosh! I looked out the window once. I saw a huge round ball of fire dropping through the air, a bomb, I suppose. I saw the flash before the report was heard. There was shrapnel bursting in the air in little flashes here and there that looked like fire flys [sic]. We could hear it dropping, too, in the street and over in the Hospital yard. I never heard anything so noisy as the alert of the can[n]ons. Six or seven go off to give the alarm. We stay upstairs until we hear the barrage. Then we leap for our slippers and coats and go tearing down the stairs. Once we get in our little wine cellar and shut the door—the noise is deadened and we don't feel half so nervy.

August 15, 1918

Dearest Family:

....Practically every night the Hun comes over bombing. If he doesn't come right over us, he does nearby. It means that we get the alert. Since our recent bad raid Alice and I prepare for anything and rush across the street at the sound of the first can[n]on. We like to go tout de suite because it is dangerous (falling shrapnel) after the barrage begins, which it does if there are any planes directly over. The place we rush to is a room underneath the band-stand in the Hospital Yard. It is not bomb proof, but a direct hit is the only thing that would get you. That chance is much better than having a whole house on your head in case a bomb hit the Hotel. It would topple over like a paper house. So each night now I put on shoes and stockings, a shirt and jersey over my nightie, arrange my coat and muffler ready to grab and hold my tin helmet in my hand. In this garb I lie on the bed trying to get some sleep before the alert. Alice and I are the first ones to reach our "abri" which ought to tell you that we are speed artists. Whether there is a raid or not we must stay there until we hear the French bugler in the street bugle the "All-Clear." It's the sweetest music in the world, "Toodle-do-doo-de-doo-de-doo-toodle de doo de doo." One awful night were two alerts and just after we had got back to our rooms and into our precious beds, we had to fly over again. My only consolation is that losing sleep does keep one's weight down! After we become accustomed to it, too, it isn't going to be so bad. I am nearly adjusted already. It seems a mere matter of course now to dress for an air-raid and rush out across the street half-clad with one's hair flying to the breeze. I do it as naturally as if I were getting up to breakfast. If there is no raid we sit outside on benches and watch the shooting stars. There are millions this month. Some nights I am so sleepy I think I'd rather be bombed in bed than move and then again I feel very wakeful. It is much harder … on the poor nurses who really need all their rest unbroken, as working in a hospital takes it out of you in nerves.

I have bought ice-cream freezers for the men. Last Sunday we had Vanilla Ice-cream with hot chocolate sauce. Ohh-la-la! ….

Did I tell you the story of the Australian patient who came to our hospital? He was full of praise for the Americans and said that just after they (the Australians) had gone over the top, the Americans came after them and caught up. The Germans rushed out yelling, "Kamerad—Got mit uns," and the Americans rushed to meet them shouting in their turn, "Keep God, we don't want him! We've got the Aussies with us!" Isn't that delightful?

There have been ever and ever so many Hun prisoners going by to-day guarded within an inch of their lives. I suppose they are some of the latest ones. Did you ever see anything like the Boche? We surprised them in our last attack and took four days to gain what they gained in one, and now they are a solid wall of resistance. Don't get too optimistic over there. The Americans just saved Paris at Chateau Thierry, but the casualities [sic] were perfectly tremendous, it is said. There is a lot more fight yet in the Hun and he is going to die kicking like Hades till the very end.

Estelle Pearl Cushman (Baldwin) (1889–1968)

Born in Hampden, MA, and raised in Hartford, CT, Estelle Cushman graduated from Yale with a bachelor's degree in music in 1914 and coauthored in 1915 (with Maude Andrews) *Songs for the Seasons: Rote Songs for Children*. After graduation she served for three years as first assistant supervisor of music in the Savannah schools. She married Arthur Lamkin Baldwin in September 1920, had two children, and became involved in the Georgia Music Educators Association and the Connecticut Music Educators Association.

In July 1918, *Musical America* stated that Cushman was the sole female "song leader" at U.S. army camps by government appointment, although an item in the *Musical Courier* of September 5, 1918, indicated that she was associated with the YMCA at Fort Screven in Tybee, GA.

"The U.S. Army's Only Woman Song-Leader Tells of Her Work"
by Clare Peeler
Musical America 20 Jul 1918: 9

. . . Estelle Cushman of Savannah, pretty, young, blue-eyed, auburn-haired, well-dressed, is as charmingly feminine in her manner and has as winningly girl-like a way as if she had never in her life done anything more masculine in its scope than tatting.

. . . "The men are crazy about singing," she said happily. "They take to all kinds that you give them and they are so grateful. No, only about forty per cent like the 'classical' kind, or rather the semi-classical. You know what I mean—music that is very good in itself and that they have heard so often that they are fond of it, as they are of some hymns, or their college songs, and for the same reason they like the Rubinstein Melody in F or the Dvorak Humoresque. So they get that kind if they like it and the 'popular' kind. I mean the good 'popular' kind. But *no 'jazz!'*"

She set her mouth firmly.

"And very little rag-time," she added. "They don't really seem to demand either one."

"Do you play for them?" she was asked.

"Oh, yes," she said. "And sing, too, of course. But you'd be surprised to find how much the men like to do their own singing, their own playing when they can. When the hot weather came on, for instance, we had to reduce the Fort concerts to one a week, on Tuesdays. So we gave the men their choice between hearing a concert weekly or taking part in a 'sing,' and they almost unanimously took the 'sing.'"

Miss Cushman begins at once to teach the men singing in harmony instead of in unison.

"It makes such a wonderful effect," she says, "so much finer than the usual unison singing. But when they first come they're so funnily bashful about it. I ask them what they sing and they generally say, 'Oh, I don't know. I just sing'; or else they say, 'Why, I can't sing anything.' Then I have each one just sing a line or so, and put him in as first tenor or second, first bass or second, and he goes off perfectly proud of himself. Presently they're singing away at part-songs as though they had known harmony all their lives. They write me the nicest little notes when they go North, 'I'm singing second tenor in the quartet. You just ought to hear me,' and that kind of thing. Of course the amount of good that comes from an interest like that for them I don't suppose it's possible to estimate. Some of the quartets we've made have done such good work, when the men got thoroughly interested, that the members have been asked to travel about the neighboring towns to give little concerts."

Author and war correspondent Mary Roberts Rinehart, ca. 1915. Library of Congress, Prints and Photographs Division, reproduction no. LC-DIG-ggbain-22942.

Born in Philadelphia and raised near Pittsburgh, Mary Ella Roberts earned her nursing qualification from Pittsburgh Training School for Nurses and interned at Pittsburgh Homeopathic Hospital. She married physician Stanley Marshall Rinehart in 1896, and they had three sons. Rinehart began publishing short stories in 1904, but her long career as a bestselling mystery and romance author launched in earnest in 1908 with *The Circular Staircase*. She and her husband are buried in Arlington National Cemetery (by virtue of her husband's army service).

As one of the earliest U.S. female war correspondents, she interviewed King Albert and Queen Elisabeth of Belgium and Queen Mary of Great Britain, toured military hospital facilities in Belgium and England, and published articles about these experiences in the *Saturday Evening Post* that became the basis for the book *Kings, Queens, and Pawns: An American Woman at the Front* (1915). Later, she obtained permission to view domestic training and hospital facilities for the army and navy that she planned to cover in future articles (such as "The Gray Mailed Fist," *Saturday Evening Post*, June 1917).

In the excerpt below from her 14-page report to Secretary of War Newton D. Baker, she describes some of her findings and recommendations after visiting Fort McPherson, Fort Myer, Fort Niagara, and Plattsburgh in summer 1917. Her August 1917 letter to Colonel Ralph H. Van Deman, a pioneer in military intelligence, highlights the anxiety that existed about enemy activity on American shores, but Rinehart the mystery writer certainly can be seen in its lines.

"[C]ommanding Officers Had Consulted My Ignorant Self on the Building of Trenches"

Report on the Training Camps at Fort McPherson, Fort Meyer [sic], Fort Niagara, and Plattsburg [sic]; also on the Training Unit at Harvard University (uncorrected)
n.d. [ca. late 1917; Rinehart visits date from summer 1917]
Special Collections, U of Pittsburgh

… FORT MCPHERSON.

Quite frankly, Fort McPherson is suffering from two things: lack of executive power on the part of the commanding officer, Colonel [Charles E.] Noyes, and lack of space. Practically all the work of the reserved officers' training camp is done by the Adjutant. Colonel Noyes is rarely in evidence, and when in conference, accepts no suggestions from his junior officers.

The result is a feeling among the men that their training is secondary in importance to the commanding officer, to the ordinary duties of the post, and the care of the German prisoners interned there.

Extreme

Extreme heat which makes the hours on the rifle range torture, since the range lies in a muggy valley surrounded by hills with rarely an air moving, lack of space, including a parade ground so small that it is not possible to gather all the men together for the ceremony of Retreat, the fact that this camp lies on the very borders of the city of Atlanta are the three physical handicaps.

As a matter of fact the question of putting any training camp in the State of Georgia as long as the age of consent is only ten years seems a very serious one. Only Georgia and Hawaii have such an age of consent. Also, although the state is nominally a dry one, drinking is quite openly countenanced at country clubs and hotels when people take their own bottles and flasks with them. It is then served by the waiters openly.

Vice conditions are not good in Atlanta. . . .

All around Fort McPherson the land is cultivated. The result is the impossibility of combat maneuvres [sic] under anything approaching conditions at the front. An officer there took me out in a machine to show me the lack of space for combat maneuvres, even on a small scale.

Hospital conditions are very inadequate—one small brick building having been made into a hospital. As Fort McPherson now accommodates regular troops, interned German prisoners, and reserve officers training corps, the sick had overflowed from the small infirmary to the upper floor of one of the barracks at a considerable distance.

Plans have been made for new hospital units to be built there. But it is respectfully [stated?] that the method under consideration by the surgeon stationed there will not make for efficiency. Surgeons are not architects, and in view of the intention to use McPherson throughout the following winter, no hit or miss construction of hospital units will solve the difficulty.

Nursing facilities are most inadequate, as is the operating room; an appendicitis [operation] going on while the room was in course of being plastered and repainted. This is not the fault of the operating surgeon but of conditions naturally arising from the new system. . . .

There is no time to teach fighting of battles by means of blackboards. As compared with the present Canadian schedule for officers training camps we have much more study, much less practical work in the field, and no trench organization such as is the most elemental necessity for a platoon leader to understand in France. We are in effect still using the combat methods of the Spanish [-American] War and there will be no time to teach these officers trench fighting in France. They will have the new army to teach and they will not have even a rudimentary knowledge of present conditions to give them.

I have said with great frankness in my previous letter that commanding officers had consulted my ignorant self as to the building of trenches. One regular officer in the artillery had built a trench—the only one of any pretentions that I saw—in sandy soil. He had made no attempt whatever to shore it up, and the result was that it caved in, injuring and burying for four minutes, three men. Yet he showed me this trench three feet deep as against 9 foot in France with considerable pride. It was necessary to bend double to get any shelter in it whatever.

. . . . [S]omehow, somewhere, we should be able to place in each camp men who know something about the new fighting.

It may be said in answer to this, that trench warfare will be taught on the other side. But if the experience of the Canadian troops as Neuve Chapelle is anything to go by, they were given, in spite of many promises, no time at all in France, but were sent direct from Salisbury Plain to the trenches. It was said at that time that they would receive their trench training at the front where the trenches were already constructed.

The result was the disastrous battle of Neuve Chapelle, for the Canadian forces were almost wiped out.

"[S]trange and mysterious events"
Letter to Colonel Ralph H. Van Deman, 2 Aug. 1917
Special Collections, U of Pittsburgh

I feel constrained to report to you a condition of affairs in my home town of Sewickley [PA]. Possibly you have already had reports about the Elmhurst Inn, a small private hotel of good class near Glen Osborne Station. I am rather inclined to think that at one time the Service had a man there.

The facts are as follows: Until some months ago the hotel was run by an American woman. At that time it was bought out by a German whose name is [not provided, but possibly A. E. Hager].

Since that time people residing in the hotel have reported at various times strange and mysterious events. Naturally in a small town it is easy to rouse suspicion and how much may be due to the fact of the proprietor being a German and strongly pro-German in his sympathies I do not know.

I am reliably informed that foreign gentlemen carrying valises are constantly appearing at this hotel, which is more of a large boarding house than a hotel and has not transient business; that these men come at all hours of the day and night, remain for a few hours closeted with the proprietor and then depart.

This has been going on for several months and comparative security appears to have made the proprietor and his visitors reckless.

The whole matter may amount to nothing whatever, but I suggest its immediate investigation. Sending an agent to live in the hotel would only rouse suspicion since, as I have explained, there is no transient business and people who come are generally well-known and fully accredited.

If you can think of any way in which I can help in this matter I shall be very glad to. If, for instance, you wish to send an agent to my house which is within a few hundred yards of the hotel, I will put him up gladly and his being my guest would remove all stigma of suspicion from him. If there is anything in this at all, it is a matter for quick work.

Marie S. Dahm (Shapiro) (1897–?)

Marie S. Dahm, Naval Intelligence Fingerprint Department clerk, Ziegfeld Follies showgirl, sportswear designer. Library of Congress, Prints and Photographs Division, reproduction no. LC-DIG-hec-10422.

Born in Brooklyn, Marie S. Dahm was the daughter of James Dahm, president of the New York Typographical Union. A showgirl with the Ziegfeld Follies of 1922 and 1923, she appeared in other musicals and won a vocal scholarship that entitled her to a free trip to Europe. She married Abram Shapiro, who headed women's garment manufacturer Mutual Rosenbloom Corp., and had two daughters. Under the name Mary Stevens, she was a sportswear designer for her husband's firm.

In April 1917, she joined the Navy as a yeoman (F) and served in the Naval Identification Bureau as a "fingerprint girl" along with Blanche Donahue of New York, and Julia G. Boswell and Blanche Stansbury of Alexandria, VA. Dahm had trained under Gertrude Sullender, the fingerprint expert at Blackwell's Island, and achieved the top score on the examination to enter the bureau—ahead of a group of 39 men—and also earned the top score on the subsequent civil service examination.

"The Making of Satisfactory Prints"
From "Fingerprint Records of Uncle Sam's Jackies to Be in Charge of These Girls" *Washington Times* 3 Mar. 1918: 3

Enter "Lady Raffles."

Right off the bat, she wants to hold your hand; she is eager to learn your address; she wants a line on you and your family; she is a regular "man hunter," but watch out—she delights in double-crossing you.

No—she is not the girl you are thinking about.

She is the "Fingerprint Girl" doing her bit for Uncle Sam. There are four of these sisters to the girl detective in Washington today.

How It Works

If you enlist in the navy, you are escorted to the Identification Bureau of the navy. Fourteenth and H streets northwest [in Washington, DC], and one of these pretty "Fingerprint Girls" takes your hand in hers and you make an impression on—a card, or you send in your card to the young lady and she files it.

Some time later, you desert, your name is changed, you alter your clothing, change the cut of your hair and otherwise disguise, but that does not fool these girls, they have your fingerprint. An officer says, "I want you," and you know one of the "Fingerprint Girls" has double-crossed you.

. . . . In their office . . . they daily locate an average of about 200 enlisted men of the navy, who in some way have evaded martial law. They are daily proving their department to be one of the most important branches of the service.

Why They Do It

When asked why they entered this sort of war work, they chorused that knitting was too humdrum, that they wanted something thrilling, so they decided to follow "The Lure of the Fingerprint," written in so many choice detective stories.

These girls can discuss whorls, ridges, and unlar loops while making a "print" as glibly as the knitters talk about "dropping a stitch" and "purling."

"I like my work as much as peaches and cream," said Miss Marie Dahm, 389 Rhode Island Avenue northwest, and the second girl in the entire country to enter work of this kind.

Thrilling? Sure!

"Thrilling? Why, I should say so! When we have succeeded in 'following up a missing' there is as much excitement as if a burglar broke in," she declared.

Miss Dahm, who looks like the original "peach of a girl," and anything but a cruel man hunter, acting as spokesman of the group, described how a print is made.

"An impression of all ten fingers is taken. A print of these is then made and turned over to a girl who classifies them, and then designs a pattern for them. Last—"

"Oh Marie, don't talk so fast. You made me draw a whorl instead of an unlar loop," spoke up one of the girls who was then making a "print."

"Last," continued Miss Dahm, "we give the print a classification number and file it."

This system is used by the Government in order that a permanent record of every recruit may be kept and in identifying an occasional deserter.

These girls can locate a criminal in five minutes through this system. The bureau has the girls constantly searching the files for duplicates, which mean that some man has done something crooked.

If he is a deserter and re-enlisted the second time under an assumed name, the duplicate on the file will betray him.

Identify Dead

Miss Marie Dahm explained that frequently dead bodies are identified through these prints. Tuscania [a troop ship torpedoed by a German sub] victims have been identified this way by War Department fingerprint experts, she said.

"The skin of the finger tips of dead bodies," she explained, shuddering, "which have been recovered from the water are greatly wrinkled and shriveled, so that without some treatment the making of satisfactory prints may be difficult, if not impossible.

Elizabeth Foxwell

"To overcome this, water is injected beneath the skin of the ball of the finger. This smooth[e]s out the skin and restores the impression to its natural condition."

. . . .[This] bureau [has grown] from 300,000 fingerprint records to 600,000 owing to the war. . . .

Ruth Bancroft Law (1887–1970)

Ruth Law, n.d. Library of Congress, Prints and Photographs Division, reproduction no. LC-USZ62-17971.

Ruth Bancroft Law earned her pilot's license in 1912, was the first woman to fly at night and loop-the-loop, and set a long-distance flying record in 1916. Also in 1916, pilot Marjorie Stinson trained Canadian aviation cadets in Texas, and aviator Leda Richberg-Hornsby was rebuffed in her attempt to serve as an army aviator.

A year later, Law tried to join the US Army Air Corps. She attracted the support of New York Congressman Murray Hulbert, but the judge advocate general held in November 1917 that women could not be accepted into the army. Law then flew on recruitment and bond drives, and was granted the right to wear the uniform of a noncommissioned soldier for these events. Her October 1917 article for the magazine *Air Travel* urged men to volunteer to fly in the service (she noted that she couldn't "go because I ain't a man"); her February 1918 article, "Let Women Fly!", followed this article.

Law rose one morning in 1922 to find that her husband, Charles Oliver, had announced her retirement from flying in the press, ending her aviation career.

Elizabeth Foxwell

"Let Women Fly!"
Air Travel Feb. 1918: 250, 284

Should women be permitted to join the United States Flying Corps?

This question has been asked of me many times in the last few months—ever since I announced that I intended to go to France and fight for Uncle Sam in the air.

There has been much controversy about the ability of women as fighters. Is it not possible for women to possess talents along martial lines, as well as in other directions? May it not be that some great strategist and tactician is now going about her household tasks, without the opportunity of putting her gifts to the proof, while warring nations are the losers thereby? When some men are forced to fight whether they want to or not and whether they have any especial ability in that direction or not, why should not women be permitted to fight, if they want to and have had any training or experience that could be utilized in warfare? The various corps of fighters would have nothing to lose by giving them a trial.

What of the thousands of women on the battle fronts to-day who are fighting in the name of the Red Cross? Are they in any less danger or have they less bravery than the men whose wounds they are binding up, well within the range of shellfire? These wonderful women are permitted to go through any danger. Their service is tireless, unfailing, heroic—yet it is considered as an integral part of warfare. Their presence on the battle-field is esteemed a necessity.

Why, then, should not other women be permitted to serve their country in the air, if their ability in that branch of the service is proven? Because women aviators would be a new factor in warfare, perhaps—but for that matter, in what other war has the airplane figured? The problem of air fighting is so totally new that there is no precedent to govern it.

Red tape and precedent—bugbears of ambition—are the two worst enemies of any country in time of war, and our good old U.S.A. is no exception. I spent many weary weeks in Washington trying to persuade the officials there that they ought to make use of my six years of flying experience by enlisting me in the Aviation Corps.

Major-General George O. Squier, who has always been one of the most progressive leaders of the Flying Corps, agreed with my views and stated that he could see where women might be of great value in the service. But he discovered on further investigation that he could not lawfully enlist a woman in the United States Army. To remedy this, a bill was promptly introduced in Congress by Representative Murray Hulbert [of New York] to permit the commissioning of women in the Flying Corps of the Army. On all sides, members of the House of Representatives offered me their support, and I began to see visions of myself flying in France and to wonder with what success I would bombard the Hun.

Then the bill was referred to Mr. [Newton] Baker, the Secretary of War, and right there, to my dismay, our old enemy "precedent" got in a "knockout blow." Mr. Baker said: "We don't want to let down the bars to women in the army."

I was disappointed because he would make no exception in this case of the air service, but I was not discouraged. Personally, I felt that it was a question of training and experience, rather than of sex, and that the world was at its old game of developing, speeding up and training its man power, while disregarding, passing over and wasting its woman power.

There is the world-old controversy that crops up again whenever women attempt to enter a new field: Is woman fitted for this or that work? It would seem that a woman's success in any particular line would prove her fitness for that work, without regard to theories to the contrary. Women have demonstrated their ability to fly by doing it, by performing stunts and accomplishing difficult feats in the air. They have the alertness, the verve and the endurance necessary to make good aviators. They do not lack courage, and they respect authority, so that they execute commands carefully, efficiently and with precision.

Women have flown; women have thrown bombs and fired guns—yes, even cannon! Then who can say that women cannot fly and fight? It is true, men do not like to think of women as fighters, but that is no proof that there are no women who are fitted to fight.

Might not a modern Polly [sic] Pitcher fly over a German town in a reprisal raid? Or a twentieth century Joan of Arc command a submarine? Or a present-day Boadicea bag a German in No Man's Land? Or a death-dealing Valkyr drive a tank crashing across trenches and villages? What of those brave and eager women warriors, the Legion of Death, who strove to re-animate the courage of the Russian host? And that was trench warfare—the most terrible kind of conflict known—that they were waging! Though no one appears to question either their bravery or their endurance, not one of the warring nations has seemed any more disposed to test the ability of its women as fighters.

But trench warfare is another story. I feel sure that the time will come when women will be welcome in the air service, just as the time came when they were permitted to enter business and the professions. Now that woman is turning her hand to everything and taking over so many kinds of "man's work," it seems strange indeed that the air should be closed to her.

To-day women are building the airplanes that the men are flying. Is it too much to hope and to believe that a to-morrow will come when the women will fly as skillfully as they now build?

Sister Florence Grace Means (1885–1968)

Sister Florence Grace Means, n.d. Photograph courtesy Daughters of Charity Province of St. Louise Archives, Emmitsburg, MD.

Born in Wisconsin, Florence Grace Means was a nurse and one of 11 Daughters of Charity who served at Base Hospital Unit No. 102 in Vicenza, Italy, also known as the "Loyola Unit" for its ties to Loyola University in New Orleans. They were the only nuns to serve with the U.S. army in the European theater during World War I. The chief nurse was Sister Chrysostom Moynahan, the first registered nurse in Alabama. According to the Daughters of Charity Province of St. Louise Archives, the staff cared for approximately 3,000 patients at the facility, and only 28 patients died. When Sister Chrysostom passed away in 1941, she was accorded a funeral with full military honors.

Elizabeth Foxwell

"A Destroyed Country"
Diary, 1918
Courtesy, Daughters of Charity Province of St. Louise Archives,
Emmitsburg, MD

Nov. 5—Bulletin published saying peace or an armistice will be signed. An ambulance goes to field hosp. where they see 2000 wounded and dying lying on cots and on the floor. Only ten of our Italian sisters in attendance. Sometimes six are found dead in the morning. Ambulance of officers and nurses go as near as they could to the firing line. Women are not allowed very near. They see awful sight of dead and dying. Bodies piled up but no one to bury the number. The soldiers remaining the hind legs of horses (that have fallen) for food. Those living and suffering from head injuries are not even taken to hospitals. Our Italian Sisters visit our hospital and are amazed at what they see such as trays, back rests, sanitary sputum cups, bed pans, etc. Our only means of heating in the kitchen is by oil stoves. They blow up at regular intervals. The soot and smoke blackens our linen in one day. Even the coal oil gives out and we are unable to heat water.

Nov. 6—Food is an awful question. The supply of corn [sic] beef and hash has been exhausted. A regular panic occurred among the patients this a.m. for black bread and straight black coffee which is their breakfast every morning. Twenty were without rations until noon and none to be had. The officers only settle the fuss with the promise that they will be served first at noon. More talk about a new medical hospital. We are unable to care for the influenza and pneumonia cases.

* * *

Dec. 14—Beautiful days of sunshine after our rainy spell. A pitiful case i[s] brought in. Young American near here in their quarters dreamed he heard the "siren" air raid whistle and walked out of a full length window of a three story building in his sleep, breaking both wrists and his nose. This was all in a dream and he didn't wake up until he was injured. Everyone is so thankful that those awful nightmares are over. Every clear night we went to bed with our clothes on in the awful horror of a night raid if it was moonlight.

* * *

Mar. 10 [1919]—At nine, three sisters, 3 nurses, one civilian and three officers set out for Mt. Grappa and the war zone near the Piave. The day is cold so we all take plenty of blankets in which to bundle up. From Vicenza we go to Citadel over the usual smooth Italian roads. Citadel is a very pretty city surrounded by a high wall as most Italian cities are. This is covered with evergreen vine which makes it beautiful. We ride around the city outside the wall. The next city we visit is Itella Franka headquarters for American troops during the war. We get an extra supply of gasoline as we are to have a hard day. From here we go to Asola where [w]e begin to see real signs of the devastation of war. The houses are bombed. We visited a house occupied by Napoleon in 1766.

After about 35 mi. of travel we reach Mt. Grappa. It is 35 mi. to the top over the road which is called the hairpin roads. It is 18 mi. straight up. The mountain is wired to the top because of the melting snow. We go up a short way. Trolleys can be seen to the top from which baskets swing in which the sick and wounded were carefully brought down. The road being steep and narrow, the ambulances without lights and great difficulty in passing. One went over and, of course, never was heard from. This and the surrounding country is territory occupied by the Austrians. Not only devastated beyond repair, all the building[s] are minus windows, doors and casings.

We went into the trenches and dugout occupied by the soldiers. They are stall-like arrangements, very close quarters, the only opening being the door. Eight or ten men occupy these dugouts. They are supported by sand bags to prevent caving in when bombed. We ate our lunch on an army blanket spread outside one of these dugouts and surrounded by nets and barbed wire. This is on the bank of the Piave.

After dinner we get into the ambulance and cross the concrete bridge destroyed at both ends and spanned by a temporary bridge. The river is only a small stream now, but when swollen is a rushing torrent. From here we go thru [sic] a destroyed country. One village after another with scarcely a stone upon a stone. We count nine churches in different villages almost flat. The Austrians knew the Italians would gather here for safety so made them targets. We passed acre after acre of ammunition piled up and left by the Austrians when they made their retreat.

We then recrossed the Piave on a pontoon bridge. There is a bridge built on boats, the rope connecting can be cut after the army crosses, so the enemy cannot follow. The men all got out and walked over this bridge. We only realize now how very near the firing line we have been all these months. One cannot help remark the thrift of the people in their reconstruction work. They are of German descent.

One would think the ground had been newly plowed from the turned-up earth. Some holes being 4–6 ft. deep. All a result of the explosion of fallen bombs. We met many ox carts bringing back the refugees to the vacant spots that were once their homes. The government doesn't advocate the return of these people before reconstruction, but it seems a case of "no place like home" even though they have been away for four years. We consider this one of our most interesting days spent in Italy.

Nellie F. Snow (1881–1963)
and Mary C. O'Rourke

The "Hello Girls" of the Signal Corps, probably ca. Apr. 1918. Nellie F. Snow is sixth from left, front row. Library of Congress, Prints and Photographs Division, reproduction no. LC-DIG-ggbain-26700.

Nellie F. Snow, chief operator for New England Telephone and Telegraph from Lowell, MA, led a contingent of bilingual "Hello Girls" to serve the AEF and cope with the less than efficient telephone system in France. As part of the Signal Corps, she ultimately was stationed in Bordeaux.

Mary C. O'Rourke left her teaching job in New York City to serve as a "Hello Girl" for 15 months with the Signal Corps' Fourth Unit in Tours and Paris.

"The Work of the Telephone Girls"
From "U.S. 'Hello Girls' in War Work Make Big Hit in Paris"
by Arthur E. Hungerford
Philadelphia Inquirer 29 Sept. 1918: 1–2

. . . . Telling of the work of the ... telephone girls in France, Miss Snow said:

First, I must say a word of appreciation to the Y. W. C. A. for its splendid work in looking out for our comfort and welfare. I do not know what we would do without it. This club [the Signal Girls Club, which housed the Hello Girls in Paris], which is really a remarkable institution, is only part of its work. Then the Y.M.C.A. dances mean so much to us and to the soldiers.

The work of the telephone girls here is much like it is at home. The life is different. We work in 7 and 8-hour shifts according to the time the work is done. We have no late night shifts, however, for the work is light then and the men take it over.

With ninety-nine girls over here we, of course, have many types represented, but the group is a remarkably fine one. It includes college girls who came over as [it] offered them the only opportunity to get into war work. They were sent to a telephone school before they came over. Then, we have a number of trained telephone operators who can speak French. Ability to speak French is not so important as it was at first.

The girls are under military discipline and observe it wonderfully well. It is hard for a girl who has been used to do almost as she pleases to have to secure permission before she can go for a walk after dark, but the girls are meeting the situation in a splendid way.

As new girls arrive from the States they will be sent to a special school so that when they are assigned to permanent duty they will be fully fitted to do the work efficiently and quickly.

I would not have missed coming for anything. I had hoped to be sent to the front, but though some of our girls are within shell range of the enemy, the army has taken every precaution to protect us.

The officers and enlisted men are kind to us. It seems that they cannot do enough for us. They are the finest men in the world.

We are the happiest women in the world, for we were allowed to come to France to do our part in winning the war.

"To Oil Ruffled Waters"
From "Impressions of the A. E. F."
Mary C. O'Rourke, *The Telephone Review* [NY]
Repr. in *Cohocton* [NY] *Times Index*, 10 Mar. 1920: 2

Together with thousands of others of the A. E. F., I found coming back to our dear U. S. and to civilian pursuits something of a jolt.

For several weeks I felt myself a misfit, even in the bosom of my devoted family, and that is how fifteen months of army life has affected my previous years of undisturbed tranquility as a civilian.

Nothing will ever efface the memory of those months in France; at every turn one finds reminders. Even the uniform is fraught with subtle memories, derived not alone from the service stripes and shoulder insignia, which, in my case, is the fleur-de-lis of Paris, scathingly referred to by the combat tro[u]ps as the "White Feather." On my dressing table is a cushion bristling with insignia of rank from Lieutenant's bars to Colonel's eagles, diminutive tanks, flying wings thoughtfully mounted on pins for a lady's convenience, gas service and staff insignia, various infantry and artillery numerals, buttons of French and British service, and even the shoulder crescent of a little Waac who was my neighbor at one time in the hospital.

While every member of the A. E. F. values and treasures his mementos of happy fellowships, there is always an inner current of sadness at the frightful scenes of suffering which always attend upon war, and which were particularly frightful in this war.

As I turn over the accumulation of papers carefully preserved in what we called a money belt, but what was in reality rather a portfolio for dearth of francs, I find lying, side by side, the first and last chapters of the great serial. The first sheet I read begs to advise "dear Madam" that Mr. [Arthur] Somers, President of the [NY] Board of Education, is in receipt of communication from Mr. [Grover] Whalen, secretary to Mayor [John F. Hylan], reading:

"The Mayor today approved the application of Miss M. C. O'Rourke, teacher, for permission to enlist in the U.S. A[rmy]." The letter reads: "On the occasion of your departure to the U.S., the Chief Signal Officer, A. E. F., desires me to commend," etc.

Elizabeth Foxwell

From Public School Teacher to Operator

. . . It was a considerable transition from public school teacher to telephone operator, from the voice with the frown, alas, to the voice with the smile—from teacher to learner. . . .

My first assignment was Tours, the charmed S. O. S. [Service of Supply] Headquarters. It came as a great disappointment at a time when all eyes were eagerly looking toward the advance sections. It has lately come to my knowledge that my family was operating upon influential friends in Washington to keep me out of range of enemy guns. However, Tours turned out to be a delightful niche for real work. I was long distance recorder, handling from 500 to 800 calls daily, and it was mine to oil ruffled waters caused by delays and by the vagaries of French Central; to squelch pert corporals demanding preferred service on highly original pretexts, or to tactfully restore calm to irate rank, or still again to firmly characterize a call from Captain X to Countess B as hardly official and therefore not to be considered.

All Kinds of Calls

Very soon "Long Distance" had become a character in the barracks life and was laughingly discussed in offices and billets as a young lady not to be hoodwinked. I recall one corporal who had long been branded in the office as a telephone nuisance. He received my statement of a two-hours' delay on Chaumont circuit with bad grace and promptly demanded preference service, which I as promptly refused. He called in frequently for reports as to the progress of his call, couching his query something like this, and in an unpleasantly whining voice, "Operator, I've been waiting 30 minutes for Chaumont; you said there will be two hours' delay. When shall I get it?" Each time I'd reply, "By arithmetic I should say 1 hour 30 minutes," always giving him an exact subtraction between the two hours and the time he had so far waited, to his infinite annoyance.

Sometimes we had an aviator in trouble forcibly landed in some French town and desiring to communicate with his Base. One day a very agitated small British voice asked with great diffidence for the "Brit-ish flying school at Vendome." He cheerfully confided his name upon request as "Leftenant . . . ."

176

but when I asked his number he hesitated. "My numbah?" he queried. "Must you have it? Wait a moment." I waited several moments after which he read off to my astonished ears a number of six figures. We had something under 500 telephones in Tours, so I wondered; argued; he assured me. We verified several times, but I was mystified until astute questioning revealed that he had given me his metal check number and, indeed, had been obliged to open several garments at the throat to do it.

I soon came to have my friends on the line. To a stentorian "This is Major [and Dr. Franklin G.] Balsh," the operator could frequently add the rest of the data, i.e., "at M. 409, calling Colonel T. Ch. and if he's not there will you speak with Major M.?" This never failed to please and was a mute witness to the prominence of the Major calling. "Long Distance" won fame as a memory expert.

In Paris

Later, I was assigned to Paris, quitting Tours on the 17th of March and remaining, like the Lady from Cork, "long enough to get the accint." In Paris I became special operator between the President's House and Elysee Palace and talked with many celebrated persons, American and foreign, among the former being Colonel [Edward M.] House, Mr. [Herbert] Hoover, Miss Margaret and Mrs. [Edith Bolling Galt] Wilson, the latter of whom always prefaced her wants with "Nice little girl, will you get me, et cetera."

Then I became "Information" at Elysee Palace, where I wrestled with questions of myriad sorts from the Czecho-Slavic situation to the probable winners in the Inter-Allied Rowing Meet on the Seine, until one day an inspired C.O. invented a phrase which alleviated my distress at falling short of omniscience. The major phrase is, "We disperse only telephone information, Sir." Fancy being asked where one may borrow a saw, or what is the rate of exchange on the Paris Bourse or innumerable questions concerning francs and centimes?

When the time drew near for the meeting of the Conference at Versailles, the men of the Signal Corps undertook the installation of telephone facilities at the Palace, and it was my good fortune to assist as "liaison" between the French and A. E. F., a task that gave me entree to the vaulted, tomblike passages under the palace, ordinarily withheld from tourists and sightseers.

It was not, however, all work and no play. The social situation was brilliant and the possibilities when on leave were boundless. No tourist will ever see France quite as did the American young lady war workers on leave. The playground of princes is open to her. The Riviera, Cotes d'Azure [sic], the gold and turquoise glory of the Mediterranean; the crystal splendor of Chamonix of the High Alps, Grenoble watering places, notably Biarritz, St. Malo, and the Spanish and Italian borders—all are hers.

Proud to Belong to Signal Corps

I cannot stop without offering the greatest tribute to the gentlemen of the Signal Corps, both officers and enlisted men. Nothing which I can say would be so significant as the fact which are a matter of statistics—firstly, the Signal Corps won a greater number of decorations for distinguished service than any other branch, and secondly, they contributed the largest sum to the war orphan fund at Christmas—exactly 78,000 francs [approximately $13,929]. These facts connote the two great extremely opposite virtues of valor and kindness of heart; one can surmise all the other intervening in the scale.

The telephone units are proud to belong to the Signal Corps. . . .

Julia C. Stimson (1881—1948)

Julia C. Stimson, ca. 1920. Library of Congress, Prints and Photographs Division, reproduction no. LC-DIG-hec-14335.

Born in Worcester, MA, Julia C. Stimson received a bachelor's degree from Vassar in 1901, graduated from New York Hospital School of Nursing in 1908, and earned an MA from Washington University in St. Louis in 1917. She served as superintendent of nurses at Harlem Hospital from 1908 to 1910. In 1911 she headed the new Social Service Department at St. Louis Children's Hospital.

Stimson was chief nurse of Base Hospital 21 (the St. Louis Unit) from June 1917 to April 1918. She was then appointed chief nurse of the American Red Cross and director of nursing for the AEF. Decorations for her service included the US Distinguished Service Medal, the British Royal Red Cross, and the Medaille de la Reconnaissance Française.

Named superintendent of the Army Nurse Corps in December 1919, she served at the rank of major in this role until she retired in 1937. She was recalled to a short term of active duty in World War II to assist in Army nurse recruitment. She received the rank of colonel by an act of Congress in 1945.

"How are we going to stand the mental strain?"

From *Finding Themselves:*
The Letters of an American Army Chief Nurse
in a British Hospital in France (1918): 78–84.

July 25, 1917

In the past 24 hours we have admitted more patients than the total capacity of the Barnes and Children's Hospital [in St. Louis]. . . . And all these patients have been bathed, fed, and had their wounds dressed. Some of course were able to walk and could go to the bath house and the mess tents, but most of them to-day are stretcher cases, and oh, so dirty, hungry, and miserable. The mere (I say mere, but it is really the most important part of the whole thing) proper recording of the names, numbers, ranks, nearest relatives, etc., is in itself a huge task. Of course the nurses don't have all that to do, but they have a lot of it. The boys who are stretcher bearers must be so lame, they can hardly move, for just consider what it means to lift down out of ambulances as many patients as that, and then afterwards carry them as far sometimes as a city block, for we filled our farthest tents to-day. It is most remarkable how things have gone. There are many aching backs to-night, for all the beds are very low and the stooping is terrific, but every one has been a brick. Many of the nurses have worked 14 straight hours to-day, and many of the doctors had only two or three hours' sleep last night, and were working all day. ….To-night things have straightened out a lot, but it is going to be a busy night as we are to send out a convoy, and get another in. Three additional night nurses are on to-night, taken from the day force that has to stretch itself a little thinner.

Our nurses don't need any "Hate Lecture" after what we have seen in the past few days. We have been receiving patients that have been gassed, and burned in a most mysterious way. Their clothing is not burned at all, but they have had burns on their bodies, on parts that are covered by clothing. The doctors think it has been done by some chemical that gets its full action on the skin after it is moist, and when the men sweat, it is in these places that are the most moist that the burns are the worst. The Germans have been using a kind of oil in bombs, the men say it is oil of mustard. These bombs explode and the men's eyes, noses, and throats are so irritated they do not detect the poison gas fumes that come from the bombs that follow these oil ones, and so they either inhale it and die like flies, or have a delayed action and are affected by it terribly several hours later. We have had a lot of these delayed-action gassed men, who cough and cough continuously, like children with whooping cough. We had a very bad case the other night who had not slept one hour for four nights or days, and whose coughing paroxysms came every minute and a half by the clock. When finally the nurses got him to sleep, after rigging up a croup tent over him so that he could breathe steam from a croup kettle over a little stove that literally had to be held in the hands to make it burn properly, they said they were ready to get down on their knees in gratitude, his anguish had been so terrible to watch. They said they could not wish the Germans any greater unhappiness than to have them have to witness the sufferings of a man like that and know that they had been the cause of it. It is diabolical the things they do, simply fiendish, and like the things that would be expected from precocious degenerates.

I cannot imagine what kind of change is going to take place in our minds before we get home. There are so many changes coming over our ideas every day. They are not new ideas, for many people have had them before, since the beginning of this war, but they are new to us. Human life seems so insignificant, and individuals are so unimportant. No one over here thinks in any numbers less than 50 or 100, and what can the serious condition of Private John Brown of something or other, Something Street, Birmingham, matter? One's mind is torn between the extremes of such feelings, for when a nurse takes the pulse of a wounded sleeping man and he wakes just enough to say "Mother," she goes to pieces in her heart, just as though he weren't only one of the hundreds of wounded men in just this one hospital.

. . . . But what will we think when we get through with it all? How are we going to stand the mental strain? Yet others do, and go on being normal, cheerful human beings, teaching bayoneting one hour, and playing tennis the next, or having tea with pretty nurses. Oh, it's a queer world! as the orderly said who came to tell me of a few more hundred wounded expected in soon. "Isn't it a cruel world?"

The Aftermath

"After Four Years of Nightmare."

Margaret Mayo, from *Trouping for the Troops,* p. 147.

Margaret Mayo (1882–1951)

Margaret Mayo with her husband, Edgar Selwyn, ca. 1911. Library of Congress, Prints and Photographs Division, reproduction no. LC-USZ62-98742.

"The Swaying Masses of Humans Below Us"
From *Trouping for the Troops* 145–47

And then came the morning of November the 11th when all ears were open for the sound of the cannon that should proclaim the signing of the armistice. I myself heard nothing, but at noon boys began parading down the Avenue de l'Opera with flags—their hands on each other's shoulders. By two o'clock the streets were swarming with men, women and children, marching aimlessly back and forth, hugging and kissing each other and sometimes trying to sing the Marseillaise.

At three o'clock when I looked down on the Place de l'Opera from the top of the Equitable Building, where I had joined friends, the streets were a mosaic of black, blue and tan, the red caps of the French soldiers with their yellow cross bars standing out like sunflowers amongst the more somber colours of the swaying masses of humans below us. Occasional vehicles overladen with shouting soldiers made their way here and there through the streets but these were few and far between and there were no bands or horns available to help out the voices that were trying to sing.

Across the street from us in front of the Rue de la Paix, it soon became the fashion for American and French soldiers, hands on shoulders, to form in long lines and march into the bar of the café for a drink.

We watched the crowds without finding much variety in their antics until the wonderful Paris twilight began to wrap the distant steeples and turrets in mist. Opposite us the victory group on top of the Paris Opera House was silhouetted sharply against the sky and just underneath it the siren that had sounded so many alarms to terrified Paris in the four dreadful years just passed, seemed to be brooding on its lost occupation and I wondered how many years it would be before all the "Cave de Secours" signs would have disappeared from over the cellarways that had so long offered sanctuary to the fleeing.

With friends of the Marine Corps I drove down to the Place de la Concorde through the Champs Elysée and into the Bois.

The guns from the submarine on the Seine were still booming their tidings of victory as we neared the Arc de Triomphe. A procession of French men and women bearing the flags and banners of the Allies swept through the splendid opening and on toward the Bois, singing the Marseillaise.

As we passed further into the Bois we saw no one save here and there a pair of strolling lovers, unmindful of any tumult, save that in their own hearts. And ephemeral things, such as war, and immortal things, such as love, seemed once again, after four years of nightmare, to slip into their rightful proportions to each other.

Anna Lewis Jones (1887-1967)

Anna Lewis Jones was the great-great granddaughter of John Marshall, chief justice of the U.S. Supreme Court, and the daughter of Thomas Marshall Jones, a physician who practiced in Alexandria and Warrenton, VA. She also was related to the Shriver family of Maryland. Jones was a stenographer for the office of the chief surgeon, AEF, and located at Base Hospital 45 in Toul, France. She owned Blue Door Antiques in Alexandria ca. 1930–38.

"It's the Environs of Verdun That Simply Hold You Spell-Bound"
Letter, Alexandria [VA] Library Special Collections

Toul, France, Dec. 18 [1918]

Dearest Mama [Elizabeth Winter Payne Jones],

I had a wonderful experience yesterday which I want to write you about while it is fresh in my mind. A very nice old general, who like all generals over here has a gorgeous limousine, took several girls and myself to Verdun. I should say it is about 50 miles from here, the roads are good and we left at 9 and got back at 6, and staid [sic] up there quite a while.

Verdun is on a hill, which is the culmination of a series of hills. You have seen pictures of old fortified cities back in the days of the Romans, well it is just like that. Part of the road we went over was built by the Romans, and it is still a superb road except where a shell hit and tore it up in places. I have been pretty much all this sector, Thiercourt, St. Mihiel, all of it, but after Verdun it looks like child's play. Destroyed villages I have seen by the dozen, in none of them is there a whole house, in some a few foundations of houses show where was once a village, or maybe a town, but it[']s the environs of Verdun that simply hold you spell-bound. For a radius of ten miles around the city of Verdun there isn't a tree, in fact in all the sector where there was fighting, the trees are shot to pieces, and this sector is almost treeless and France is so beautiful forested, if a Frenchman cuts down a tree he plants another, and they are planted with a great idea to beauty and effect, but around Verdun there are miles and miles that were once great forests and not a tree, in other areas where there was farmed land, the earth looks like I imagine places look after an earthquake, turned upside down, there was constant fighting there for four years and as you know the French always held Verdun, it was considered a great strategic point, but I don't suppose they could have held out much longer, the Americans never fought there you know. In some places the once superb road . . . was so torn up from shells that it was most difficult for the machine to navigate trenches and dugouts and . . . shell holes big enough to get a house in, from German 30s shells, like the ones they used on Rheims, those great big fellows. The boys can tell by looking at a house or wall, which was hit, the size of the shell, whether it was a 75 or 105 or a 305 pounder. You see for miles and miles in this country, you always seem more or less on a plateau, it['s] mountainous, but not a ridge which obstructs the view like the mountains at Warrenton. . . . .Of course we did not even get out and walk over the land any, in the trenches the mud is to your neck and that is what the boys lived. In the dugouts is still in many instances gas, always rats and cooties [lice], but the dugouts run all along under the hills. There are millions of little places dug in the earth just large enough for a man along the hillside, and that is where the boys dug themselves in during terrific shell fire, and there they would be until the shelling ceased, sometimes for 24 hours or more.

We rode through both sides, first the area occupied by Germans, then the immense stretch of land which was no-man's land, then the French area. You know they shell sometimes at a distance of 20 or 30 miles and can hit any spot they aim at, it's a mathematical problem to me how they pick a certain village, say from 30 or 40 miles and shell or gas it (gas shells) but we learned to do it too, and shelled many villages in order to get the Boche out. We shelled Chateau Thierry too, and I believe the policy is for us to pay for the villages we had to shell. Our boys are working all along the roads trying to restore. It[']s one way to keep them busy till they go home.

The one thing that strikes you in all the advanced zone and area where they fought is that there is not a woman to be seen, in Toul and Nancy are the only places where you see a woman, though now a few refugees are coming back, but of course they have no houses to come to[.] Fliry, not far from here[,] was once a good[-]sized town and now there are two walls and a few chimneys standing. You see none of their houses are built of frame, there are no frame houses in France[;] they are all stucco, so there is always a few bricks and a little stucco left standing around. We were out of the shelling area, only field hospitals were in where shells dropped, so I am just now since the fighting has ceased allowed, when I get a chance, either a truck or machine, to go to the lines, and I have been about all over this sector. All the area is now being what we call salvaged, barbed wire taken down, and there are tons upon tons of it because each side all along the lines had barbed wire, and it isn't a fence like one might imagine, it['s] acres covered with it. . . . [A]long at various places now you see salvage dumps and there are regiments detailed to the work. They collect everything, sort it, and I suppose the French will get the iron, brass, and stuff, and there is millions of dollars worth of it around.

Most all this sector has been pretty well gone over, at least a good part of it, but around Verdun, they haven't commenced and everywhere you look are empty shells and duds galore, a dud is a shell that from a faulty fuse did not explode and if you are wise you don't attempt to touch it, they have special soldiers who know the game to go over the fields and pick up the stuff, but for years to come French farmers going over the land with plows are occasionally going to meet a dud buried somewhere, and then goodbye f[ar]mer, plow and all. The empty shells, especially the 75 pounders, make lovely vases when polished and engraved with the name of the place they have come from, among the soldiers French and American of course, jewelers and etchers and artists and everything and some of them have done some of the most beautiful work on them you can image. . . . I have a German prisoner working on one which I will send to some of you.

I will tell you of the city of Verdun. It must have been a beautiful city, the canal of the Meuse runs through the city and it sort of [u]ndulates. . . . [T]he city is built on hills, a good many of the walls of the houses and stores remain. . . . [B]ut there is not a house or even a room in a house left, it['s] like a skeleton city. . . .[U]nder the city is called the Citidal [sic], or underground city where live 8,000 soldiers. . . . . [I]t somewhat reminds you of a New York subway, the walls are brick, painted white, the whole place electriclighted like day, steam heated. There are miles and miles of corridors, and great long rooms. There is a beautiful chapel, a huge bakery, barracks where the soldiers sleep, Red Cross recreation rooms, mess halls where they eat, everything you can think of. It was conceived of as a last resort in case the Boche took the city. These poor people they lived with a rapacious enemy at their throats all the time. I was most fortunate in seeing all this, we at home have no idea of what war and the feeling such as existed between Germany and France is, in my opinion France intended sooner or later to get Alsace-Lorraine back. . . .

I was most anxious to get up to Metz . . . but our A.E.F. officials have issued orders against Americans going into Metz, so I am cut out. You see there are over 2 million Americans here in the A.E.F. and now the war is over they want to get leave of absence and travel and it does not suit G[en]. Pershing or the French authorities. . . .

I don't know when we will be home, the 2nd army is still in this sector. . . sometimes it[']s a very lonely existence, very hard to get to know anyone. . . . . I am dying for something good to eat, Army food gets pretty tiresome, salmon, goldfish as the boys call it, beef, from America, sometimes I am not sure it is not horse meat as the French eat it, potatoes and tapioca figure extensively in our diet, but it[']s been a great show and I would not have missed it. . . .

Addie Waites Hunton (1872–1943)

Addie Waites Hunton. From The Crisis, *Mar. 1921, p. 205.*

Born in Norfolk, VA, Addie Waites was educated in Boston and Philadelphia and taught at the future Alabama Agricultural and Mechanical College. In 1893, she married William Alphaeus Hunton, a YMCA official involved in services for black youth in the South.

They had four children, two of whom survived into adulthood. She became a secretary of the YWCA and worked on programs for black students. Her husband died of tuberculosis in 1916. She later served on the executive board of the Women's International League for Peace and Freedom and became a vice president of the NAACP.

In summer 1918 Hunton was one of only a few black women sent to France with the YMCA to provide services for some 200,000 black troops. Hunton, with her colleagues Kathryn Magnolia Johnson and Helen Noble Curtis, worked at canteens designated for black service-men and set up educational, recreational, and other programs for them.

"Reburying the Dead"

From *Two Colored Women with the American Expeditionary Forces* (1920), pp. 233–39

. . . .[S]pringtime had come again in France with its song-birds and blood-red poppies, and with it the quick consciousness that the dead lying en-masse on the battlefields must be given resting places befitting heroes.

Here was a tremendous task for the surviving American soldiers, but far more sacred than tremendous. Whose would be the hands to gather as best they could and place beneath the white crosses of honor the remains of those who had sanctified their spirits through the gift of their lifeblood? It would be a gruesome, repulsive and unhealthful task, requiring weeks of incessant toil during the long heavy days of summer. It also meant isolation, for these cemeteries for the American dead would be erected on or near the battlefields where the men had fallen. But it would be a wonderful privilege the beauty and glory of which would reveal itself more and more as the facts of the war should become crystallized into history.

Strange that the value of such a task did not gather full significance in the minds of all American soldiers. Strange that when other hands refused it, swarthy hands received it! Yet, perhaps, not so strange, for Providence hath its own way, and in those American cemeteries in France we have strong and indisputable evidence of the wonderful devotion and loyalty and the matchless patience and endurance of the colored soldier. The placing of this task—the most sacred of the whole war—in his hands may have been providentially planned. It may have been just another means, as against the force of arms, to hasten here at home the recognition and enforcement of those fundamental principles that for four long years had held the world in deadly struggle.

We looked upon these soldiers of ours—the splendid 813th, 815th and 816th Pioneer Regiments and the numerous fine labor battalions—as they constructed the cemeteries at Romagne, Beaumont, Thiencourt, Belleau Woods [sic], Fere-en-Tardenois and Soissons. We watched them as they toiled day and night, week after week, through drenching rain and parching heat. And yet these physical ills were as naught compared with the trials of discrimination and injustices that seared their souls like hot iron, inflicted as they were at a time when these soldiers were rendering the American army and nation a sacred service. Always in those days there was fear of mutiny or rumors of mutiny. We felt most of the time that we were living close to the edge of a smoldering crater. At Belleau Woods the soldiers *en-masse* banished some who mistreated them. We recall an incident at Romagne. Even though it was May the nights were winter cold, so that when one snuggled between army blankets in the tent, it required a bit of heroism to crawl out. This particular night we had just retired when shots were heard, fired in rapid succession. Without thought of the cold we began dressing and were sitting wrapped in cloak thinking rapidly about what was happening when someone called, "It is only a fire!" What a relief it was! What did it matter if the whole camp burned in comparison with our boys being goaded by prejudice beyond reason! Rations were often scarce and poor at Romagne because we were so far from supplies, hence we prepared and served food for the soldiers all day long. But this was but a small task compared with that of keeping the men in good spirits and reminding them again and again of the glory of the work they had in hand. Always, whether in the little corner set aside in the Y barracks as our reception room, or among the books they liked so well to read, whether by the side of the piano or over the canteen, we were trying to love them as a mother or a dear one would into a fuller knowledge and appreciation of themselves, their task and the value of forbearance.

We had gone from Romagne—women of fine spirit had taken our place and were lovingly ministering to the needs of these soldiers, when things happened too grievous to be calmly borne. At one stroke down came tents of discrimination and injustice, but the work there went on and the soldiers completed the difficult task assigned them.

For weeks at Romagne we watched these men fare forth with the dawn to find the dead on the 480 square miles of battlefield of the Meuse-Argonne. At eventide we would see them return and reverently remove the boxes from the long lines of trucks and place them on the hillside beside the waiting trenches that other soldiers had been digging all the long busy day. Far into the night we would sit in our darkened tent looking out on the electric-lighted cemetery, watching the men as they lowered the boxes into the trenches. Sometimes we could hear only a low murmur of voices, and sometimes again there would come to us a plaintive melody in keeping with the night hour and its peculiar task.

....May we not hope that as the heart of this homeland finds its way to those American shrines in France, a real peace, born of knowledge and gratitude, shall descend upon us, blotting out hate and its train of social and civil injustices? Then shall we realize the value and meaning of the pain and sacrifice of these dark-browned heroes of ours.

Winifred Holt (Mather) (1870-1945)

Winifred Holt teaching checkers to blind officers, ca. 1915. Library of Congress, Prints and Photographs Division, reproduction no. LC-DIG-ggbain-20653.

The daughter of publisher Henry Holt, Winifred Holt trained as a sculptor, producing works that included a bas relief of Helen Keller and exhibiting in Berlin, Florence, and New York. After observing some blind boys at a concert, she founded an organization that distributed tickets for theater and music performances to the blind. She and her sister, Edith, subsequently established the New York Association for the Blind (later known as Lighthouse International) to provide job training to the blind and education on blindness. During World War I, she set up an affiliated organization in France to assist soldiers blinded in the war, followed by a similar organization in Italy. For her work, the French government bestowed on her the Legion of Honor, and the Italian government awarded her a gold medal.

In 1922, she married Rufus Graves Mather, who joined her in expanding Lighthouses for the Blind to countries such as Japan and China.

"The Horizon of the Educated Blind Man"
Letter, From *First Lady of the Lighthouse* 88–89

Hotel de Crillon
July 9, 1915

Dear Mr. [Joseph H.] Choate:

I know you will be happy to learn that your letting me come over here has been an unspeakable boon to the poor men blinded in battle. While the government reports officially 1800, I have been told unofficially by public officials that there are actually about 20,000 men who have lost their sight. These poor souls remain hopeless and desperate in hospitals.

We have already founded one Lighthouse—"Le Phare [lighthouse] de Bordeaux"—for the blind men whom I found there in the hospitals. We were able to reorganize a little organization which existed there without funds but with a most able, intelligent director, l'Abbé Moureau.

The government and thus far everybody whom I have met is enthusiastic about our mission and eager for our aid. If we had a million dollars—this is no exaggeration—we could change the entire situation for the blind of France. We can alleviate it with a little sum at our disposal. Any money, therefore, which you can get will be more than welcome.

In the hospital the other day I found a desperate young officer who had been there for months. He had lost both eyes and his left arm. His right one had been horribly mutilated, but two fingers still remained. I talked to him of the Lighthouse and of the horizon of the educated blind man, and pointed out to him that on his mutilated right arm he still had two eyes—his two remaining fingers—with which to play games and to read. He smiled, for the first time I believe since his accident; and said: "Mais oui—I may then still be useful."

There is literally nothing being done in the hospitals for the blind men. I am now organizing a corps of able teachers to take them light while they are still in physical incompetence and mental misery. Tomorrow I go to state my case before the Cour de Cassation, and have already the sympathetic ear of the Department of the Interior and the War Office. The government is giving us Frs. 2.50 a day for the food of our men in the Bordeaux Lighthouse.

I can never be sufficiently grateful that we have the privilege of helping here, but I beseech you to let it keep on. They will soon need us more in Italy than they do here.

Elizabeth Robins (1862–1952)

Elizabeth Robins, n.d. Library of Congress, Prints and Photographs Division, reproduction no. LC-DIG-ggbain-02745.

Born in Louisville, Elizabeth Robins was an actress before she turned to writing plays and novels and supporting the women's suffrage movement. *The Convert* (1907), *Ancilla's Share* (1924), and "Where Are You Going To?" (1912) are some of her well-known works. She moved to England in 1888 and worked for a time during World War I in London's Endell Street Military Hospital that had an all-female staff. She contributed the following piece to *Reveille*, the quarterly journal edited by John Galsworthy to highlight the plight of disabled servicemen.

Elizabeth Foxwell

"Soldiers Two"
from *Reveille*, Feb. 1919: 378–82

When I think of the difficulty confronting those who have in hand the tasks set forth by *Reveille*, I am reminded of two types of soldier who would never be cured by the same machinery. They represent for me the two poles of the same problem. One of those men will never want to do anything so much as to talk about his new experiences. The other will not tell you enough for you to help him.

With the first my acquaintance began and ended in a hospital ward. He was there a long time, and for long he was too weak for talk. He whispered and gesticulated; nothing could keep him quiet except morphia. When his conversation became more audible, I was horror-struck at this fragment that reached me as I passed: "That cuckoo of a doctor." He hailed a convalescent who halted his wheeled chair to hear. . . . Yes, the sick man was at it again—complaining. Not a comforting grumble, which does the patient good and no one any harm. This was a sly, laughing mockery. "That cuckoo of a doctor."

With my pile of books on my arm, I hurried past. I always hurried past that bed. Examples of courage all around me and not an ounce of it in my heart. Here was a case still too serious to need the ministrations of a librarian, yet not too serious but what strength could be found to undermine confidence in the hospital. He talks like that because the surgeon is a woman, I decided. The man didn't know his luck. And so, when the long, clay-coloured face looked out at me over the bedclothes, I could find it in my heart to be glad that, in addition to his wound, he had some trouble with his eyes. I needn't try to find out whether he preferred [Arthur] Conan Doyle to Jack London, or whether he was one of those agreeable "finds" who would ask you wistfully if you had a poetry book or something about "Exploring."

Those were the early days of the war. But we librarians had already been taken into the confidence of certain soldiers for whom we had written letters, or done some trifling service. "When us chaps found they'd sent us here, we thought we hadn't a dog's chance. We ain't worth bothering about"—and that was why they'd been sent to the Women's Hospital.

We watched that opinion change, as convoy after convoy passed through those four-and-thirty wards. We saw how the spreading confidence helped the hordes of wounded newly come.

And now, here was this grey slum-product, with the lifeless wisps of straight black hair hanging over a damp forehead; his weak eyes seeing everything; his long-lipped mouth with not one upper front tooth left, uttering disaffection; restless, talking, for ever talking. On the smallest provocation, or none, he would shoot out a skeleton arm to fumble in a back-handed way behind the locker-curtain. Out he would bring a horrible little bag of trophies; the nozzle of a bomb, some battered souvenirs, two German buttons. He would tell the story that belonged to each, and by an implacable sequence go on to describe how he got his wound, and how "that cuckoo—"

The back of my forbearance broke the day he engaged a newcomer in the next bed.

"Why do you call your doctor a cuckoo?" I demanded.

"*Was* a cuckoo," he said, laughing that toothless laugh. "You see, I was hit just—"

"Yes, yes"—I knew about the dreadful business.

"An' this cuckoo of a doctor took five pieces of shrapnel out o'me. Five. *An' never gives one of 'em back!*"

"Oh, that's why—" I began to turn over in my mind the possibility of letting the doctor know how she had outraged the passion of ownership for metal fragments which had been carried with so great inconvenience in the hero's vitals.

"I said to him: 'Is that all there is?' Yes that cuckoo of a doctor at Boolong I'm tellin' you about. 'I ain't sayin' but there's more,' says 'e. 'There *is* more. But that's all I'm going to meddle with.'"

And then at great length the pleasing of the cadaverous patient and the flat refusal of the Boulogne surgeon to operate any further. "I says to the lady when I come 'ere—." And then, if you could fancy such a thing, you were to believe that the patient had explained the exact situation and what the surgeon was to do. "I got to have it out, lady," I says. "It ain't worth me thinkin' o' goin' home with that shrapnel worrin' me inside like that." He'd much rather die and be done with it.

The lady had said the Boulogne surgeon was right. The irritant fragment *was* in a bad place. "But we'll feed you up and get you to sleeping better, and then we'll see."

Again that motion I'd grown familiar with. The bony forearm shot out of the covers, and plunged behind the curtain. "And now you can see! She don't go chuckin' away other folks' belongin's. Not she! Had it there, all ready for 'em to show me, when I came round."

He fished out of his calico bag a ragged piece of iron. He pointed out a yellow stain. "Poison, that is. Think o' carryin' that home in your gizzard 15,000 miles. I says to that cuckoo in Boulong: 'I come too far, doctor, and I got too far to go to be carryin' that about.'"

I looked at the slum face. "Where do you live?" I asked.

He named an island in the South Seas. Eighteen years ago an enterprising Lancashire builder had accepted a contract for a bank and a block of offices to be erected in the principal town. Among the workmen taken out, my clay-faced friend, then sixteen or seventeen, "thought it'd be good for me 'ealth." He had prospered, done a little contracting on his own account, married, had several children, felt himself a pillar of the little community, consisting of 1,200 British in addition to the native population. The first ship, that took to those remote shores the news of August, 1914, sailed home with volunteers. "How many" did I think took that first chance to go and fight a battle 15,000 miles away? That 1,200 British included babies and old men, women and children. How many did I think came back to fight with the first ship? *"Fifty of us able-bodied men.* That's twenty per cent of our population. By the first ship. I says to that cuckoo—"

In return for his story I told him how on my first trip back from America after England declared war, the Atlantic liner was crowded with British: men from Manitoba and the farthest North; ranchers from Texas and Colorado; professors from the colleges; business men from everywhere, leaving their material advantages behind them, like my South Sea islander—steaming home along all the lanes of ocean....

We talked about what that stood for. And often we had spoken of the hold England had upon her sons. We spoke of English gentleness. I told him if I hadn't learned before what the English tradition stood for, I would have learned it in that hospital—from soldiers. It had fallen to me to know the plain people of a good many lands. I could compare.

I tried to make him see the significance of that miracle of good feeling and good manners which had brought success out of a gentler rule than military hospitals had ever tried before. We knew something of the record these men (all sorts and conditions, mind you) had brought from the battlefields. It couldn't beat their record here. We'd heard about Kultur. But we had seen here in this hospital a civilization of the spirit, which was perhaps the thing best worth keeping alive in the world.

I drove a bargain with the South Sea islander. He was to add this miracle to his war experiences, and I would spread abroad the story of the English in the Pacific. His delight when I came back and said I had been talking about him to a county magnate, who had found the South Sea story one of the most effective passages in his recruiting speeches. "That fifteen thousand miles of yours has shortened the distance to the nearest recruiting station for more than one man!"

He smiled his toothless smile: "Pity your friend couldn't have shown 'em the piece of shrapnel; that cuckoo said he didn't dare——." He had the bag out in a trice, and the trophy on the counterpane. "I've been wanting to ask you. How'll I have it set? Silver, or gold?"

I thought silver. But he inclined to gold; he pointed out it would match the poison stain. It would also go "with me watch chain."

I could see it, dangling. I could hear him leading the conversation round to it all the way back to the South Seas.

It might be well if the majority were as direct, as simple, as ready to let us "share." Such men will be easier to help than a certain Sussex gardener.

A man of medium height, compactly built, with Norse blue eyes, and a slow smile. After many many months of hospital, he was beginning to get back his fine country colour, doing odd jobs in my garden. Not from him—from his wife—I heard of the awful blowing away of flesh and muscle from back and arm. Between elbow and shoulder the arm was no bigger than her wrist. A number of operations had left him with a wound which still swelled and discharged, a wound which the young wife had to dress morning and evening. Twice a week he must needs go to the hospital. When I understood his condition better I knew he oughtn't to do any but the very lightest work. I told him so. He seemed to agree.

When I came home I could see he had done a great deal. I asked what I owed him. He submitted a paper setting forth the work, and a wholly inadequate charge. I pointed out the self-evident fact.

"I can't ask what I would before the war," he said, making his first reference to the fact of his service. "I don't call myself able-bodied now."

I learned his method of work, how he managed to use a heavy, clumsy wheel-barrow, by means of a cord round his neck and the one strong arm. I heard of his rolling the lawn. All done with one hand, he assured me. From an upper window I happened to catch sight of him, rolling the turf above the drive, where it narrowed to meet an iron fence. I saw him struggle with the heavy roller, as it all but ran off the foot-high turf to the gravel. Both hands on the bar, he pulled the weight back. I ran down to speak to him.

It hadn't hurt him; did him good. Took some o' the stiff feelin' out.

I interrupted him. "Oughtn't you to carry that arm in a sling?"

I thought he looked a little "conscious," and stubborn too. "Don't they tell you at the hospital?"

He mumbled: "Oh! the hospital!"

Then I took him to task. He ought to do what his doctor told him. He could wear the sling part of the time anyway.

He wouldn't answer.

But his wife did. "He won't wear a sling," she said resignedly. "He says when he wears a sling people takes too much on theirselves [sic] with sympathy."

Sophie Irene (Simon) Loeb (1876–1929)

Sophie I. Loeb, bet. 1915 and 1920. Library of Congress, Prints and Photographs Division, reproduction no. LC-DIG-ggbain-20935.

Born in Russia, Sophie Irene Simon emigrated to the United States as a child and resided near Pittsburgh. She married Ansel Loeb, the owner of a store in which she was employed, in 1896; the couple divorced in 1910. She became a reporter for the New York *Evening World* and president of the city's Child Welfare Board, and was the first woman to mediate a strike. She later became an ardent supporter of the Zionist cause.

"The Returning Colored Soldier"
Evening World 7 Dec. 1918: 10

…Never in the history of the world has the colored race played its part with such heroism as on the fields of battle in France. Many a marvellous [sic] incident has been recalled by the leaders. Reporters have come from the other side and gloried in the recital of the noble work done by the colored race. While the new day is dawning and we are preaching democracy in the day of brotherhood—let us practice it. Let us give opportunity to the colored soldiers who return.

Reconstruction means in their direction as well as in the case of his white brothers. ...[A]ll reconstruction comes right down to the individual. There can be no real reconstruction in the world's work unless the individual plays his particular part.

Playing his particular part means giving the chance rather than charity. When the colored soldier comes back and seeks work of you, Mr. Employer, squelch your possible prejudice for his color and say to yourself, "He fought for me while I remained at home. He took the chance to die. Is it not up to me to give him the chance to live, the chance for livelihood?"

All any honest man of any color or creed wants is this opportunity to make his way. It does happen that sometimes because of his color he does not get a job as readily as his white brother.

No better time than the present to reflect on the fact that God made us all.

The color line should certainly never be drawn to the strangling point, if the world would surely be safe for democracy.

This anonymous Yeoman (F) letter writer was apparently responding to "Expect Women Yeomen to Lose Jobs Soon," an unsigned piece in the *Brooklyn Standard Union* of 15 December 1918 that attributed laziness, vanity, and high salaries to the female yeomen at the Brooklyn Navy Yard and asserted that "until the women get out of the navy 'things will never run right'" (5).

"A Reply to the Attack upon the Yeomanette"
Brooklyn Standard Union 21 Dec. 1918: 4
repr. *Evening World* 21 Dec. 1918: 10

Brooklyn, 17 Dec. [1918]

To the Editor of *The Evening World*:

Do you remember when war activities were at their height, the flattering articles written about the "yeomanette" and the work they were doing? How they [sic] answered the call for women to enlist to carry on the work left unfinished by civilian clerks who had gone to the front?

Now that demobilization is in progress these same clerks fear that their old positions will not be restored to them, we having proven ourselves capable. (Our capability may be verified by the numerous recommendations for re-rating.) Therefore, the method taken by them of belittling us to the public by writing articles, we consider despicable.

Contrary to the statement "that the officers were anxious to discharge us," a commander of the Fleet Supply Base was heard to remark: "If the entire office forces consisted of yeomen (female), then the work would be conducted satisfactorily."

Then too the critic mocks us for "assuming the dignity of officers." We would ask what better example is there for us to follow than that of a naval officer? Would he have the women who are wearing the uniform of the United States Navy act otherwise than dignified?

We would call your attention to the fact that ridiculing a United States uniform is considered an act of disloyalty. Therefore, when he ridicules the "fancy capes and hats worn by the yeomanettes," designed and approved by Government officials, he places his judgment above that of Government representatives.

As for the complaint, supposedly made by uniformed men, that the women have "snaps" [an easy job], it is a well known fact among us that officers driven by the necessity of completing work have repeatedly detained the yeoman (female) as late as 10:30 P.M. Is this the critic's idea of a "snap?"

Later, when they needed us to fill the vacancies caused by the detachment of sailors from their despised clerical positions to active sea duty, we responded, "a woman worker for every fighter."

Elinor Sachs (later Sachs-Barr) (1895?-1990)

In April 1921, representatives of the Council of Jewish Women's European Reconstruction Unit sailed for Europe. Rebekah Bettelheim Kohut chaired the council's Committee on Reconstruction. The director of the unit was Celia L. Strakosch, and staff members were Clara Greenhut, Elinor Sachs, and Margaret Paukner. In Antwerp, the Hague, and Rotterdam the unit assisted Jewish emigrants en route to the United States and connected with local women's organizations so that these groups could eventually take over the unit's work. Paukner was assigned to the Joint Distribution Committee in Paris to serve Jewish war orphans.

Elinor Sachs graduated from Barnard College in 1917. She married David Barr; they had a daughter, Winifred, who became an economics professor at MIT. Sachs helped to organize a 1923 congress of Jewish women that was held in Vienna. She later worked for the Consumers Advisory Board, the National Recovery Administration, and the Works Progress Administration.

"Befriending the Emigrant"
From "The Council Unit: How It Served Europe"
The Jewish Woman Jan. 1922: 3–4

"This is indeed a Yom Kippur for us," she sobbed. She was a widow, scarcely 35, with two young children. Truly the world was a cruel and hostile place to her. . . . .

Mrs. Arnskoff came to the port of Rotterdam on her way to Canada. She was Russian and traveled on a passport obtained from the Russian Consulate in Bucharest, Roumania. For a whole year she had been on her way, hiding here, waiting there. From Kiev to Constantinople where, along with thousands of others, she suffered untold misery; from Constantinople to Bucharest. Her uncle in Canada sent her money to come to him. But when at last she got to Rotterdam, her passport was declared invalid for Canada. And black despair came upon her. Where was there hope for her? Where could she turn? Surely it was impossible to go back to Russia! It was equally impossible to stay in Rotterdam or to go on. She felt like a hunted hare.

With some misgivings, I set about to find out the opportunities which other countries of immigration could offer. A Jew wants to go where there are other Jews. She had a trade—she was a milliner—but she had two children and almost no money. The Ukrainian "pogromszchikes" had deprived her of both husband and worldly goods. For technical and other reasons there was only one place to go—to Cuba.

"It will be not Yom Kippur, but Rosh Hashanah," I told her in proposing that she go to Cuba. "It will be a new life and a new hope." She was polite but sceptical. Alone, to a country she had never even heard of. Yes, she had the courage to start a new life and to work hard. But, alone in a new country—. That frightened her.

In other port cities there were similar cases, of refugees whose avenue of escape was cut off. I connected up with some of these groups. Mrs. Arnskoff joined a group that was going to Cuba. Life is often more romantic than fiction, for Mrs. Arnskoff found herself among her "Landsleit"—several families from her own city. And now, in the midst of friends, she started out for her new home, with hope and thankfulness. When I went to the boat to see her off, she said: "Do you remember saying to me, 'This will be a Rosh Hashanah?' With God's help it *shall* be a New Year for us."

What the Reconstruction Unit meant to Mrs. Arnskoff, it mean to many, many others. It rendered service; it showed the way to emigrants who were bewildered or in distress. Its work will continue through the local organization which we created or the existing organizations which we quickened. We came to Holland in all humility to start a piece of work; we have left it with appreciation and admiration for the Dutch Jewish women who have taken hold of the responsibilities of the task which we pointed out to them—the task of befriending the emigrant who passes through their gates.

. . .[I]t will be in place to mention several aspects of this work. The first might be called preliminary Americanization. The emigrants in the port city who had to wait either during the normal quarantine period or for money or on account of temporary illness—their waiting time we could make useful to themselves and useful to their intended home. Teaching English—of course but a little—was a minor part. The greatest value was perhaps an intangible one. We had the satisfaction of finding that our precept and example gave the impressionable emigrant the right spiritual attitude toward America. We also spread the gospel of bodily cleanliness.

A logical consequence of the "Americanization" work was the development of emigrant aid service. When I asked one of the younger girls why she did not fill in her spare hours by studying from the English book I gave her, she retorted that her head was too full of worries to admit of anything else. It was to alleviate these worries, wherever possible, that we soon found it necessary to initiate case work. Both types of work were done along with the Dutch Jewish women, whom we succeeded in organizing. The Joodsche Vrouwenvereeniging [Serbian Jewish Women's Association], having been shown the way and methods, has taken over the work in admirable fashion. As Mrs. Jacob Kann, the distinguished president of the organization, said, "You have opened our eyes; you have shown us the way. We thank the American Jewish women for sending us this Reconstruction Unit. We assure them that we will not fail in our duty."

The Council's contribution is bigger than the mere establishment of organizations in Holland or Belgium. Through the connections we have made with the various splendid European women's organizations, we have been the unconscious spreaders of intranational goodwill. "We look to you American Jewish women to take the initiative in re-establishing the solidarity, good-will and mutual helpfulness which existed before the war." Thus shall we be rendering an immeasurable service.

Elizabeth Shepley Sergeant (1881–1965)

Elizabeth Shepley Sergeant, passport photo, 1918. Yale Collection of American Literature, Beinecke Rare Book and Manuscript Library.

Born in Winchester, MA, Elizabeth Shepley Sergeant graduated from Bryn Mawr in 1903 and resided in Paris for a time. She published *French Perspectives* in 1914. Sergeant contributed to the *Century*, *McClure's*, the *New Republic*, *Scribner's*, and other periodicals and was a member of Bryn Mawr's Service Corps that aimed to provide workers to war organizations. While on assignment for the *New Republic*, she was seriously injured during a battlefield tour in France when her guide picked up a live grenade. Her book born from this experience was *Shadow-Shapes: The Journal of a Wounded Woman, October 1918–May 1919* (1920).

She moved to New Mexico in 1920; published a novel, *Short as Any Dream* (1929); and wrote biographies of Robert Frost and Willa Cather. Sergeant's sister was Katharine Sergeant Angell White, fiction editor of the *New Yorker*, and her nephew is the baseball writer Roger Angell.

From "'Nothing Is Lost': Reconstruction and Evacuation in Northern France"
The Century Oct. 1918: 721–32

On est tout de même content d'être de nouveau chez soi —
"One can't help being glad to be at home again."

This phrase was a sort of Greek chorus to my journeys across liberated France last autumn and winter. It was poignant enough when one heard it in ruined barn-yards, in villages that looked like a cross between Pompeii and a Western mining town. For home meant little more than a piece of French earth cut by old trenches, crumpled by shell-fire, or devastated by deliberate enemy hands; a piece of earth that had come down to the owner from generation to generation, or been bought by the savings of a lifetime. There might or might not be a fragment of a house on it; but the house mattered less than the land. Now we have been hearing the phrase again in the Paris stations from the people driven out once more by the new German offensive: "We were so glad to get home again." The French peasant is the most local creature on earth. He will look with a cold eye on the snow-clad Pyrenees, on the green fields of Normandy, or on the red sails of the Breton fishing port to which the fortunes of war have assigned him, remembering only the ugly, smashed-up little village in the Somme which he has had for the second or third time to leave behind.

A woman with whom I stayed at Noyon last October gave me a description of the German retreat of March, 1917, as we had breakfast in a kitchen the windows of which were still without glass. She apologized for the lack of a table-cloth; the Germans who had occupied her house for a time had taken her linen to make ropes to dry their boots on. They had also taken the clothes of her husband, who was mobilized, and her crockery; but she had been more lucky than some of her friends, for she still had most of her furniture. That was because it came from her grandmother, and was too heavy to be moved. It was not often, she said, that they had demanded the food provided by the Belgian Relief Commission; but her eight-year-old girl looked scarcely six and showed other signs of undernourishment.

Noyon was before the war just one of the many sleepy old French provincial towns, with an hotel de villa, and a cathedral, and little gray streets twisting out into a rich, green agricultural plain; now it will always be remembered as the town nearest to Paris—only sixty-five miles away—where the enemy stayed for two and a half years. It had been used during the occupation as a sort of concentration center for the French populations evacuated from the actual firing-line. Before the retreat, however, virtually all the useful members of the community had been deported: all the men between sixteen and sixty—there were a good many of territorial age not mobilized during the first days of the war, and therefore caught by the German invasion,—and most of the women between the same ages except those who had dependent children. It was, then, a community largely made up of women and children and of the very old, who, on a certain Thursday in March, were ordered to go into their houses, close the shutters, and not come out for forty-eight hours. Promptly a series of explosions began, very alarming explosions, which made the poor people inside tremble. What new horror were they up to now? The sounds went on for a day and a half, gradually growing fewer on the second morning. By afternoon, strangely, nothing whatever could be heard; not a voice, not a rumble. The boldest spirits pushed open the shutters a little and perceived that the streets were absolutely deserted; the gray-green soldiers were nowhere to be seen. Slowly and cautiously, halting at every step, they ventured out and up into the center of the town, coming back with the astonishing news, the news that nobody dared believe, that the Germans were gone. They had blown up the bridges, burned a few factories, cut down trees along the roadsides, and made off. Even then the French inhabitants believed there must be some trick about it; and when their own soldiers, looking unfamiliar in blue uniforms instead of the old red and black, entered the town the next morning, they tried, in the midst of the tears and welcomes, to hold them back lest they get caught in an ambush. But they were again free citizens of France.

But the war was not over. As I heard the story in far more vivid detail, to the late captives the significance of this blasting fact came home to me. Of course the war would be over when the Germans left, they had argued. For this end it had been possible to endure almost any degree of suffering under the eyes of hated conquerors; but to go on for another year, or two or three, still separated from daughters, young girls now prisoners on the other side of the line, husbands in bondage or at the French front, still living miserably in exile, crowded into somebody else's house with somebody else's furniture, how was this to be endured? The French government answered the question by allowing the exiles to return to their own villages wherever possible, providing them with temporary shelter until permanent rebuilding could be done; and the relief societies of France and America and England answered it by sending out groups of workers with stocks of furniture and clothes and animals to help them make a fresh start. It was thus that devastated France became liberated France; it was thus that the land which the Germans had reduced to a desert became again a place where life, though lived close behind the battle-line, was almost normal; a place where the power of mere destruction was denied by a whole new series of creative efforts.

"The line of reconstruction should always follow the fighting front," said Mme. de S——— at the end of our lunch, such a delicious meal as only a French woman could have conjured out of a country altogether without resources, under the shadow of the gaping factory at Athies, near Péronne; and the French captain and the lawyer-poet who had come together to gather the rehabilitated farmers of her village into a cooperative agricultural society applauded her words.

This courageous young woman had lost her husband during the first year of the war; her father, an elderly sugar manufacturer, for three years a prisoner in Germany, had just been repatriated. Their chateau, their factory, the village houses, had been deliberately destroyed by fire. Only skeleton walls remained standing, and in the factory bent and tortured machinery. Virtually all the trees in the town had been cut down. But Mme. de S——— had returned, had secured portable houses from the Government, had encouraged a certain number of the inhabitants to come back, helped them to clear their land, and had settled down with her children and her father in the midst of this desolation. She said that she no longer saw it at all; what she perceived was the vast number of things there were to do. And, as I followed her slim, black figure through the ruins, I realized that she spoke truly. The ministry of labor had promised to help rebuild the factory next year. The army hoped to be able to assist her with teams of soldiers and a tractor plow.

"When France is rebuilt, it will be by the women," said her father, rather sadly, and Captain de Warren again agreed. It was the peasant woman, he said, who saw the advantages of the group activity in which he was interested.

All through the Somme and Oise and Aisne French women like the Marquise de S——— were establishing themselves last summer. Sometimes, like Mme. F——— at Lassigny, they returned to a wooden shack built on the wreck of their own homes. One lady at Babeuf came back to a country house still intact and full of excellent furniture, only it did not happen to be hers! Some German general had preferred another variety. The women who came as representatives of relief societies were usually not natives of the region, but their spirit in either case was the same—the spirit of the social settlement in the best sense. More than furniture, live stock, seeds, the people of liberated France needed friends who understood what they had endured for three years, who realized that they were not "charity cases" in the sense that the immigrants in our big American cities often are, but self-respecting citizens requiring only a little fraternity and a little material aid to get them on their own feet again.

It was the delegate of the American Red Cross at Noyon who gave me my first sight of the Oise and Aisne, and as we drove in his car from one village to the next I was amazed to see how much had already been done. We went to many places named in the recent communiqués—to Ribécourt, for instance, where two ladies of the French Red Cross had established a dispensary in a half-repaired house. There was a sick soldier in the front room, and a prize rabbit in the courtyard, and the nurses' bedrooms were almost roofless; but we were treated to a fine glass of Madeira in the little kitchen where good things were cooked for the sick children of the village. The Red Cross delegate was a favorite.

In the most unpromising backyards, by wells which were still polluted, we found women weeding rows of lettuce. Though the Germans had cut down many of the fruit-trees, the people had managed to collect a store of apples, and were making cider in presses improvised from material taken from the old trenches. We passed villages where school-houses were being set in order by elderly *instituteurs,* who rejoiced to be getting to work again. Green and red wooden *barraquements* [barracks] were springing up everywhere; but it must be said that the natives regarded these with a very unfavorable eye. They much preferred living in a piece of an old stone cellar of their own, like rats in a familiar wall. In one place a French lieutenant, a contracting architect in private life, was rebuilding three villages with a hundred German prisoners. He had a forge and a carpenter shop in full blast, where the late destroyers, now clad in verdant green, with "P. G." on their backs, were earnestly engaged in forging hinges and locks, repairing furniture and making mattresses, sawing out window-frames and patching doors. Nobody but such rebuilders as this loquacious Frenchman and the relief workers can appreciate how complete was the destitution of the country. Pioneers have at least forests to draw on; here the armies and the Germans had swept the country bare, and now the railroads and the motor transport had first to serve the *Poilus* [French infantrymen] in horizon blue, whom we met everywhere winding over the roads with their convoys of guns and supplies. The lieutenant had to make even his nails, he told us.

Ribécourt had been destroyed by shellfire; so had Lassigny; so had Tracy-le-Val, a once beautiful, gray little village that now lies almost as flat as Delphi, with the same sort of red and blue flowers growing between the stones. We passed miles and miles of no-man's-land, such as those stretches between Noyon and Vic-sur-Aisne, where the few trees that remained were mere specters, and slumping trenches and barbed wire, red with rust, crisscrossed into the distance. In contrast the German graveyards rose insolently on the hillsides, surrounded by high marble walls, led up to by marble steps, adorned with tombs carved from French mantelpieces, rustic benches made of French trees, hedges and rose-bushes transplanted from French gardens. They looked as if the Germans intended to stay forever, we said to one another, little dreaming that they would be back again. The French had surrounded these graveyards with wire to prevent their desecration. There had been quite enough of burning and sacking already. You might go into a blacksmith's shop and think, "Here is at last something that escaped." Then you would discover that the leather had been cut out of the bellows, and the anvil smashed with a hammer. You might see a farm-cart standing in a barn, but when you examined it, you found that the wheels had no spokes or the spokes no rim. At Ham the French officer in charge of agricultural work took me to see a great dump into which the Germans had thrown hundreds of plows, wagons, and agricultural implements and set fire to them. Behind it was another forge, another carpentry, and another paint shop, where French soldiers were busy making new wheels, forging new parts. "It is wonderful how many of them can be repaired," said the officer. "The love of the French peasant for his soil is more than a match for the hatred of the *Boche*." A whole row of nicely painted wagons stood ready to be given out to villages and cooperative societies.

The French army's part in reconstruction was first to fill up the trenches and to roll up the miles and miles of barbed wire. The blue-coated Territorials who guard Lassigny were engaged in these slow labors in the cold mists when I spent a few days there in December. They were, as the two French Red Cross nurses of the "Village Reconstitué" said pityingly, *pères de famille*, middle-aged men who had been separated from their families for too long a time. That was probably why in the dusky hour between five and six all the children of Lassigny might be seen hurrying with some sort of can or sauce-pan toward the soldiers' mess. The *pères de famille*, before they retired to the subterranean caves built in the hill-side that sheltered them for the night, shared their evening soup with the inhabitants, a proceeding, of course, strictly against the law. But what would not a French *Poilu* do for a family that was willing to come back and begin life over again in Lassigny? The same children between eight and nine in the morning came with milk-cans to the *dispensaire*, which, with its blue paint and gay flowered trimmings, looked like a sort of Noah's ark come to rest in a country destroyed by flood. Between the soldiers and the nurses, the children of Lassigny were fast forgetting the past.

The old first-line trenches ran straight through the town. The inhabitants spent forty-eight days in their cellars under French bombardment before they were evacuated in the autumn of 1914, living on raw wheat, on such vegetables as they could conceal in their cellars, and such bread as their kindlier captors gave them. Of the German common soldier one said, "*Ils ne sont pas plus mauvais que ça*" [They are not as bad as that]. All the same, it was at Lassigny that a boy of fifteen knocked over, entirely alone, all the monuments in the German soldiers' graveyard. A soldier had killed his pet horse wantonly before his eyes in September 1914. He had struck the soldier, and had been punished with prison, and his first act on getting back to his native village in May 1917 was to lay low the monuments, which, by the way, were statues that the Germans had looted from the fine Gothic church.

The schoolmaster at Lassigny was having a rather hard time with boys who had been running wild for three years. This was a feature of the German invasion that I had not thought of. Here were boys and girls of ten or twelve who had almost or altogether forgotten how to read and write, because they had not seen a French book or a pencil or pen since the war began. The schoolmaster had other duties, too. He was the *remplaçant* [substitute] of the *maire* [mayor], and when there appeared at his portable *mairie-école* [town hall-school] a woman from Bordeaux who wished to find the grave of her son, he was of course obliged to hand school over to his daughter and start out into the desert with the woman from Bordeaux. For three whole mornings they searched before they found the grave—in a shell-hole.

This woman slept at the other end of the dispensary ward where I was also living. The *infirmière-major* said that she kept a sort of hotel, for there was no other in the town. Our ward was a cold place. All the coal was being saved against the arrival of a woman who was expecting a baby; but it was my stay under this heart-warming roof that finally convinced me that reconstruction work back of the front was worthwhile. To see the main room of the *dispensaire* crowded with seventy-five women from all the surrounding villages on a Thursday afternoon, making themselves clothes, listening to the phonograph, drinking tea, talking of the future, was to realize that community life had begun again; and when I now think of the place as a heap of charred ruins, of the lately restored population of Lassigny as scattered through the interior of France, I feel convinced that even more than after the first evacuation they will want to come back when the war is over, and know that they have a community to come to.

If my journeys with the Red Cross delegation were fruitful in the knowledge they brought of the "social service" and relief aspect of the reconstruction work, my three days of motoring with Captain de Warren's mission gave me a profound of something still more vital to the peasant of northern France—agricultural reconstruction. The real purpose of the French Government in repopulating the region back of the front was, aside from the moral and psychological elements already mentioned, to get the soil back into cultivation. The German strategic retreat had freed more than a thousand square miles of the richest land of France. The ministry of agriculture and the ministry of war accordingly combined on a program the basis of which was the cultivation of these vast spaces with tractor plows run by teams of militarized agriculturalists. They pushed their ideas, with a program for cooperative effort, taking first the farm, then the village, then the town. This was normal reconstructive progression, Captain de Warren argued. Little more than temporary shelter could be provided until the end of the war. Material was almost impossible to get, and labor still more difficult in this zone of military activity. The idea which existed in America that model towns could spring up behind the front during the war never for a moment prevailed on this side of the Atlantic.

For two days Ham was Captain de Warren's center—Ham, the first considerable town of the Somme to fall into German hands in the battle of Picardy. The hotel, the proprietor of which was a prisoner on the other side, had never been cleaned up since the Germans left last year. I wish them joy in their return to this hostelry. The Chateau-fort, almost as fine an example of the medieval fortress as Coucy, had been very thoroughly dynamited. Otherwise the town had suffered little, although the Boche had spent his leisure hours in digging for treasure in the cellars, to judge by one where I was escorted during an air raid, a baby raid compared with those we are now used to in Paris. Yet the trenches were only a few miles away. Occasionally we saw a few German *avions* in the blue sky, surrounded by little white puffs of exploding shrapnel. But we scarcely believed in the battle last October, so absorbed were we in the soil. Even the captive sausage balloon to which I drove out after dark had *petits pois* [peas] and *salades* planted about its anchoring ropes. So do they grow about all places where the French soldier makes his semi-permanent abode.

The Somme was a region of rich, flat fields of wheat and sugar beets, of dull brick villages, which look peculiarly forlorn in ruin, in contrast to the Oise and the Aisne, where the lovely contour of the hills, the shining turn of the rivers, the soft gray of the stone, give a certain charm to devastation itself. But the few big farms in the Somme that escaped burning were fine to see. I have been thinking these last days of one where we stopped, an old stone manorial farm built about a hollow square. The courtyard was crowded with Poilus in fatigue-caps, sitting cross-legged about the fires, drinking their wine. The low-ceilinged kitchen was crowded with ancient, ancient men, dominated by the widowed mistress of the farm, discussing agricultural expedients.

"Pool the land," urged Captain de Warren; "it's the only way. The Government and the army will send you tractors and teams of soldiers to drive them, and when the army moves on, you can buy the tractors for a song, and continue the work for yourselves."

The old men shook their heads despairingly, but madame spoke up with a decided, "We'll put it through." She did, and I have a conviction that her tractor was saved and that she rode out behind it on a Red Cross truck.

The Red Cross Bureau of Reconstruction and Relief was organized last August under the direction of Mr. Edward Eyre Hunt, who had been an aid[e] to Herbert Hoover in Belgium. He divided liberated France into five districts, each with at least one field delegate, men of high caliber, some of whom had also had previous experience in Belgium. The delegate was in effect a liaison officer and lived in his motor-car from early morning till late at night, driving from *sousprefet* [subprefect] to *maire*, from *maire* to French *commandant* or British town-major, from relief unit to relief unit, finding out what their needs were, what their plans were, and what the Red Cross could do to help with money and supplies. A chain of warehouses and camionettes [vans] was gradually established from Arras to Soissons. When Lassigny needed pumps to clear out its polluted wells, it was the Red Cross that provided them. It was the Red Cross delegate at

Amiens who established a sort of factory where all the material used by the *ouvroirs* [workrooms] supported by the Red Cross were cut. It was the Red Cross delegate here or there who reported to Paris that this village needed rabbits and that one sheep, and this one spades and that one seeds. During the long invasion the name of America had already become dear to the inhabitants of northern France. What more natural than that Americans should still be patrolling their villages?

The work of the bureau was designedly indirect. It undertook only one piece of rebuilding, or, rather, temporary repairing. Five villages in a particularly rich agricultural region about Croix-Molignaux were being set in order as a sort of laboratory experiment. At Gruny, Golancourt, and Ham, units of the English and American Friends [Quakers], allied with the Red Cross, were patching roofs and windows and helping out with agricultural work. No task was too menial for the Friends, though a great part of them were college graduates, and they had probably done more for the land than any *one* other American group. The American Fund for French Wounded at Blérancourt, partially financed by the Red Cross, had done some successful repair work in a series of villages on the Aisne. As to medical aid, the Children's Bureau of the Red Cross had established a twelve-bed children's hospital at Nesles, the Pavillon Joffre, and by its traveling dispensary regularly visited seven of the surrounding villages. The Smith College [Relief] Unit at Grécourt, whose difficulties and successes during a hard winter are already familiar in America, became affiliated with the Red Cross in January. It had a doctor and nurses, and also a traveling store that took the place of a shop in many a village that lacked one, providing utensils, clothing, and seeds.

The growth of an understanding is a delicate thing to estimate in normal times, but a crisis shows exactly what it amounts to, and the part played by the American Red Cross during the offensive in March is a tremendous testimony to the strength of the foundations of cooperative sympathy established during the past seven months. In one brief and terrible week the whole of a year's work in liberated France was swept away; in one week the Germans were again at Ham, at Nesles, at Noyon, all but at Amiens and Compiègne—both of which they attacked with fierce swooping aeroplanes, armed with chains of bombs, and with a hail of shell-fire. In one week Major Hunt's lieutenants had emptied their warehouses for the benefit of the French civilian refugees and the soldiers of the Allies, and had with their own cars and camions [trucks], with the cars and camions that the American relief societies in the region at once put under their command, with more motor transportation and tons more of supplies rushed up from Paris, helped the French civil authorities and the English and French officers in the orderly evacuation of the civilian population, and the evacuation of streams of wounded, and in feeding these outgoing and incoming hordes at the rail-heads and junctions. Red Cross doctors and nurses, too, hurried toward the battle. It was an admirable piece of emergency work, and perhaps did more than a great many months of quieter labors to establish America in the hearts of her Allies. Women as well as men played a great part. Many were the young girls who ran their cars under fire to save "their people."

Major Hunt established emergency headquarters at Compiègne the first day, from which he patrolled his line of outposts from Arras to Soissons. Compiègne, already evacuated, was totally deserted of civilians, but bristling with military activity. A rolling Red Cross kitchen on the very spot where Joan of Arc was captured served from ten to twenty-five thousand British, French, and American soldiers a day. Those who merely tore by, hungry and gaunt, received from an American clergyman standing in the midst of the mad traffic chocolate, cigarettes, and condensed milk. They caught the bundles on the fly as the trucks dashed past. The once famous and luxurious hotel was taken over by the Red Cross. Some nurses of a hospital unit that had been driven from its own base did the cooking, serving all the while at the canteen and giving emergency aid in the salon to the wounded who were always being brought up the blood-stained steps. Few were the hours they stole for sleep at night in the hotel cellar. Still closer to the fighting-line in the very midst of the guns, some American doctors had stuck by an evacuated hospital were giving invaluable medical aid to desperately wounded men, while cavalry,—French cavalry, British cavalry, and American cavalry, too,—blocking the enemy's road to Paris, were saving the day with their sheer fury and their sheer determination. This was the intensest center of the Red Cross aid so far as the army went.

The civilian population was meanwhile withdrawing in the other direction, on Montdidier, on Beauvais, driving before it the precious livestock so hardly acquired, pushing wheelbarrows and baby-carriages full of blankets and clothes.

The exodus of civilian refugees has already been too many times described in this war to need repetition. The evacuation of liberated France had a peculiar poignancy, and was distinguished from other exoduses by its admirable order and its high morale. This was an élite already purged with an almost Greek purgation. The Red Cross followed up its vigorous help along the way as far as the train which took the people toward Paris and the provinces; and at the Paris stations Red Cross men and women were again waiting with the French societies, with the sympathetic French police to give food, to give lodging, to give comfort and hope.

The fugitives were particularly glad to see American faces, grateful for human kindliness, and very careful not to ask for special favors. Perhaps nothing touched them so much as the care the American girls gave their domestic animals. Few cows got as far as the Gare du Nord, but one goat which had nearly caused a family of twelve to be captured by the Germans became a famous figure, and at least one kid is said to have been born there. And the dogs! One poor widow who had four helpless woolly pups, obviously of most plebeian origin, clasped to her breast, stands out in memory, and the delightful old woman with a blooded fox-terrier of voracious appetite. "He never was so greedy at home," she explained apologetically as he emptied the plate for the fifth time. A member of one Red Cross bureau had the pleasure of taking home to his mother at midnight a little boy of nine who had come all by himself from Amiens, some thirty-six hours on the way. The superstition that an organization like the Red Cross cannot "take an interest in details" was denied at every turn.

Farther on, in the country regions to which they were assigned, the évacués were again met by Red Cross delegates already experienced in the art of making the poor exile feel at home in a strange province. All winter the repatriés who knew no "freedom" in March 1917, having remained on the German side of the battlefront, have been pouring back through Switzerland and Evian, often a thousand a day; and the bureau directed by Dr. Edward T. Devine, formerly of the New York School of Philanthropy, has been collaborating with the French civil authorities in meeting and establishing the convoys in the interior of France. The late "liberated" are, alas, only a fraction of the inhabitants of northern France who are longing for a definitive return.

Has this redevastation of the liberated region retarded or disintegrated the eventual return? Will the desert be now more likely to remain a desert? By no means. It is the liberated who will prove the leaven in the numbed masses of the refugees. When Paris newspapers advertise, for the benefit of scattered citizens, the establishment of a "municipality" like that of Rheims in a place of safety, the very advertisement proves the strength of the entity. A community like Péronne, which migrated two hundred and fifty strong to southern France, secreted by its mayor and vowed to inseparability, will be a tonic influence to repatriates who have known neither the pangs nor the spurs of homesteading. The liberated realize that houses can be rebuilt, that devastated land will bear anew, that even goats and furniture will be again forthcoming.

This is also the attitude of the French governmental authorities. These will probably be questions for government loans and interallied finance to solve. But meanwhile the Red Cross, at the request of and in collaboration with French architects, sanitarians, industrial, social, educational, and agricultural experts, is again laying foundations. This time it is by means of a campaign among refugees for better housing, healthier living conditions, more effective domestic economy, improved agricultural and industrial methods. Unless measures are taken to make rural life more attractive, and in particular to improve agricultural methods, there is danger after the war, with the decrease in manpower, of something like an agricultural crisis. Therefore movies, traveling lecturers, journalism, toys, tracts, photographs, and, most convincing of all, a fascinating series of pasteboard models reproducing prize designs by French architects of model farms and villages in the purest style of the different regions of the North, are to bring home to the *évacués*, wherever they are, the advantages of modern civilization. It is consoling, while the *Boche* is still battering down beautiful old walls, while shells are whistling over Paris, to think of a quiet band of Franco-American experts meeting together on Saturday mornings to plan for the future of a finer and richer northern France.

Dorothy Walton (Binder) (1894-1980)

Dorothy Walton, 1916. Image courtesy of Mary Mikkelson.

Dorothy Walton, daughter of Minneapolis real estate developer Edmund G. Walton, graduated from Wellesley College in 1915. During World War I, she worked for the American Friends Reconstruction Unit in France. She later became a reporter for the labor union newspaper *The New Majority*. In 1920, she married Carroll Binder (later foreign editor of the *Chicago Daily News* and editor of the *Minneapolis Tribune*); their four children include former *New York Times* reporter David Binder.

Elizabeth Foxwell

"Coming Home"
Service 1.2 (1919): 7.

Three, four, almost five years they have waited to come home. Somehow it is always impressive to me—the passionate love the French peasant has for his own bit of country, the longing he has to be there and only there. He comes back with the long hard years of privation and homesickness behind him, only to face new privations. Anything to come back. I have seen them living in dugouts, sleeping on soldiers' abandoned cots (and you know the French weakness for comfortable beds), living in the most utter misery of filth and cold. They come back to find their ancestral homes smashed to bits, their lovely old furniture either gone or ruined, only their land left and that torn up in trenches and dugouts. And the arrival must be like the experience one has of coming home after death has visited one's family. Things are changed and the familiar memories crowd so fast that one loses courage and heart in remembering the happiness of the past. It must have been like that for a family we met coming home to its village one day last spring. We were passing Dombasle, one of the Mission centres, where the Verdun train passes through, when a poilu [French infantryman] waved frantically at us and asked if we could give him and his family a lift of some five miles. The camion was already stacked with supplies for the shop at Fromereville, but we tucked the tottering, white-capped old lady in the front seat, numberless sacks and boxes were wedged in the back, and the poilu's sister and I perched perilously on the nubbly edges of things. The poilu decided to walk. Sister was in deep mourning—I gathered for the sake of style, for she told me that happily none of her family had been lost in the war. She was not a cheerful soul. We started up the main street of Dombasle, which was badly damaged. Sister saw a friend on a doorstep. "Bonjour, Marie," she called. But Marie only turned and stared at the retreating camion, not recognizing the figure in the back. Tears came to the woman's eyes. "Pauvre petite Dombasle," she sobbed, as we looked back on the forlorn little village. But when we passed a cemetery, she broke down altogether and wept whilst the old Grandmere in the front seat told the chauffeur that she had counted all the cemeteries since they had started on their journey and this one was the fortieth. As we came closer to their village they began to recognize their beloved land.

"See our apple orchard," Sister called out to Grandmere, and she sighed and unmercifully cursed the Germans, alternately crossing herself as we passed a roadside crucifix. Finally, we rattled into what was left of Bethlainville, their village. It was with difficulty that Sister was restrained from jumping out long before the camion stopped. Violently she waved her hand as she caught sight of a neighbor and tried to remember whether it was Lucille or Renee. We drove up to her house and the pent-up feelings burst into uncontrolled sobbing. To be sure her house was comparatively untouched. One might even observe that she had a great deal to be thankful for. But if one understands what it means to a French peasant to be away three long years and then find one's smiling village in ruins one is very silent. We helped them out with their bundles.

"How much?" they asked.

"Nothing," we said, "we are glad we could help you."

They did not understand. French people scarcely ever understand the "something for nothing" attitude.

We left them standing forlornly in the road by their bundles. The old Grandmere seemed not to comprehend that she was at home again, while her daughter, her face working with emotion, stared hopelessly at the ruin about her and the problem of starting life over again. The chauffeur's eyes were decidedly moist as we climbed in again and drove off to Fromereville.

WORKS CITED

Adams, Harriet Chalmers. "Luneville Feels Crushing Hand of Hun Invader." *National Geographic* Nov.–Dec. 1917. Repr. *Berkeley Daily Gazette*, 2 Mar 1918: 3. Print.

Allard, Leola."Unofficial 'Mother' Adopts Officers at Rockford Camp." *Chicago Examiner* 10 Sept. 1917: 4. Print.

Baker, Newton D. Letter to Mary Roberts Rinehart, 16 Jul. 1918. Special Collections, U of Pittsburgh, SC.1958.03. Retrieved from http://digital.library.pitt.edu/u/ulsmanuscripts/pdf/31735062227461.pdf

Bly, Nellie [Elizabeth Cochrane Seaman]. "Nelly [sic] Bly in Trenches—Die Like Flies of Cholera—Men Kill Unseen Enemy." *Washington Herald* 8 Dec. 1914: 3. Print.

———. "Woman Writer Describes Trip on Hospital Train." *Washington Herald* 13 Jan. 1915: 5. Print.

Bradley, Amy Owen. *Back of the Front in France.* Boston: Butterfield, 1918. Print.

Brown, Alice Barlow. Letter to the Woman's Committee of the Wilmette Guard. 25 Nov. 1917. Letters from World War I Collection, Wilmette [IL] Public Lib. Retrieved from http://history.wilmettelibrary.info/65159/data?n=16

Carey, Miriam E. Letter to Julia Robinson, secretary of the Iowa Library Commission. *Iowa Library Quarterly* Apr.-May-Jun. 1918: 87–88. Print.

Catton, Bruce. "Women War Veterans Reward for Bravery." *Ogdensburg* [NY] *Journal* 20 Jul. 1937: 10.

Cromwell, Gladys. "Realization." *Poems.* New York: Macmillan, 1919. 52. Print.

Dickson, Emma Young. Letter to Mary B. Dickson, [Apr. 1918]. U of Minnesota UMedia Archive. Retrieved from https://umedia.lib.umn.edu/node/665198?mode=basic

Doty, Madeleine Z. "Half-Starved Mothers of Germany in Revolt Over Food 'Red Tape'" *New York Tribune* 3 Dec. 1916: 6. Print.

"Dr. Brown Will See France from Plane." *The Lake Shore News* (Wilmette, IL) 17 Jan. 1918: 1, 6. Print.

Farnam, Ruth Stanley. *A Nation at Bay: What an American Woman Saw and Did in Suffering Serbia.* Indianapolis: Bobbs-Merrill, 1918. Print.

"Fingerprint Records of Uncle Sam's Jackies to Be in Charge of These Girls." *Washington Times* 3 Mar. 1918: 3. Print.

Higonnet, Margaret, ed., with Susan Solomon. *Letters and Photographs from the Battle Country: The World War I Memoir of Margaret Hall*. Boston: Massachusetts Hist. Soc., 2014, Print.

"Homes Are Asked of Hoover for U.S. Women Veterans." *Washington Post* 8 Aug. 1931: 9. Print.

Hull, Peggy. "Peggy in Paris Describes Her First Terrorizing Experience with Murderous German Planes." *El Paso Morning Times* 2 Sept. 1917: 7. Print.

Hulsizer, [Edith] Marjorie. Letters. 15 Sept. 1917, 26 May 1918, 15 Aug. 1918. Hulsizer Family Papers, Library of Congress, Manuscripts Div.

———. "Miss Hulsizer Writes Another Interesting Letter from 'Somewhere in France.'" *Hunterdon* [NJ] *Republican* 4 Jul. 1917: 1. Print.

Hungerford, Arthur E. "U.S. 'Hello Girls' in War Work Make Big Hit in Paris." *Philadelphia Inquirer* 29 Sept. 1918: 1–2. Print.

Hunton, Addie Waites, and Kathryn M. Johnson. *Two Colored Women with the American Expeditionary Forces*. Brooklyn: Brooklyn Eagle P, 1920. Print.

"Jean Eliot's Chronicles of Capital Society Doings." *Washington Times* 24 Nov. 1918: 14–15. Print.

Jones, Anna Lewis. Letter. 18 Dec. 1918. Special Collections, Alexandria Library, Alexandria, VA. Print.

"Junior League Girl Drowned Off Liner." *New York Times* 18 Jun. 1925: 1. Print.

Law, Ruth. "Let Women Fly!" *Air Travel* Feb. 1918: 250, 284. Print.

"Legion Starts Fight for Service Women." *Philadelphia Inquirer* 16 Sept. 1923: 2. Print.

Loeb, Sophie Irene. "The Returning Colored Soldier." *Evening World* 7 Dec. 1918: 10.

Mather, Winifred Holt. *First Lady of the Lighthouse*. Ed. Edith Holt Bloodgood. New York: The Lighthouse, New York Assn. for the Blind, 1952. Print.

Mayo, Margaret. *Trouping for the Troops: Fun-Making at the Front*. New York: Doran, 1919. Print.

National War Work Council. *Summary of World War Work of the American Y.M.C.A.* New York: YMCA, 1920. Print.

"Needy Women Veterans." *Evening News* [NY] 7 Jul. 1925: 4. Print.

O'Rourke, Mary C. "Impressions of the A. E. F." *The Telephone Review* [NY] Oct. 1919. Repr. in *Cohocton* [NY] *Times Index*, 10 Mar. 1920: 2. Print.

"Passports to Go to France Issued to but Few Women." Committee on Public Information *Official Bulletin*, 29 Jan. 1918: 4. Mary Roberts Rinehart Papers, Special Collections, U Pittsburgh, SC.1958.03. Retrieved from http://digital.library.pitt.edu/u/ulsmanuscripts/pdf/31735062227461.pdf

Paul, Maury. "Tragedies of Society: Cromwell Clan Trailed by Jinx." *Milwaukee Sentinel* 24 Dec. 1939: 5C. Print.

Peeler, Clare. "The U.S. Army's Only Woman Song-Leader Tells of Her Work." *Musical America* 20 Jul 1918: 9. Print.

"Plan Hospital for War Women." *Pittsburgh Press* 30 Mar. 1928: 11. Print.

Purviance, Helen. "A Doughgirl on the Firing Line." *The Forum* Dec. 1918: 648–56. Print.

"A Reply to the Attack upon the Yeomanette." *Brooklyn Standard Union* 21 Dec. 1918: 4. Repr. *Evening World* 21 Dec. 1918: 10. Print.

Rinehart, Mary Roberts. "The Gray Mailed Fist." *Saturday Evening Post* 23 Jun. 1917: 11+. Repr. *War Readings*. New York: Scribner, 1918. 243–50. Print.

———. Letter to Colonel Ralph H. Van Deman, 2 Aug. 1917. Special Collections, U of Pittsburgh, SC.1958.03. Retrieved from http://digital.library.pitt.edu/u/ulsmanuscripts/pdf/31735062227487.pdf

———. Report [to Newton D. Baker] on the Training Camps at Fort McPherson, Fort Meyer, Fort Niagara and Plattsburg; also on the Training Unit at Harvard University. Mary Roberts Rinehart Papers, Special Collections, U Pittsburgh, SC.1958.03. Retrieved from http://digital.library.pitt.edu/u/ulsmanuscripts/pdf/31735062227487.pdf

———. "The Woman Behind the Soldier." *McClure's* Apr. 1918: 5, 32, 56. Print.

Robins, Elizabeth. "Soldiers Two." *Reveille*, Feb. 1919: 378–82. Print.

Rohe, Alice. "Healing Mutilated Italian Soldiers by the Power of Suggestion." *Norwich* [CT] *Bulletin* 3 Oct. 1917: 12. Print.
———. "Italy Keeps Its Troubles Secret." *Urbana* [IL] *Daily Courier* 13 Aug. 1915: 3. Print.

Root. Esther Sayles, and Marjorie Crocker. *Over Periscope Pond: Letters from Two American Girls in Paris October 1916–January 1918*. Boston: Houghton Mifflin, 1918. Print.

Sachs, Elinor. "The Council Unit: How It Served Europe." *The Jewish Woman* Jan. 1922: 3–4. Print.

Scidmore, Eliza Ruhamah. "Japan's Platonic War with Germany." *The Outlook* 23 Dec. 1914: 914–20. Print.

"Serbs Call for Women Physicians." *Pittsburgh Press* 14 Sept. 1919: 3. Print.

Sergeant, Elizabeth Shepley. "'Nothing Is Lost': Reconstruction and Evacuation in Northern France." *The Century* Oct. 1918: 721–32. Print.

"She Nursed Our Wounded at Chateau-Thierry." *New York Times* 28 Jul. 1918: 37. Print.

Sherzer, Josephine. Letter. n.d.. *The Michigan Alumnus* Jan.1919: 251–52. Print.

Stimson, Julia C. *Finding Themselves: The Letters of an American Army Chief Nurse in a British Hospital in France*. New York: Macmillan, 1918. Print.

"Tapering Off the War." *Goodwin's Weekly* 14 Dec. 1918: 6–7. Print.

Tappert, Katherine. Letter to Julia Robinson, secretary of the Iowa Library Commission. *Iowa Library Quarterly* Apr.-May-Jun. 1918: 107–08. Print.

[Thiebaud, Gertrude]. "Work in a Hospital Library." *Library Occurrent* Oct. 1918: 83–86. Print.

Walton, Dorothy. "Coming Home." *Service* 1.2 (1919): 7. Print.

Waters, Crystal. "A Singing Girl in No Man's Land: How I 'Entertained' Our Boys during Their Battle for Thiancourt." *Sunset* Jan. 1919: 40–42. Print.

Women's Oversea [sic] *Hospitals U.S.A*. New York: National American Woman Suffrage Assn, 1919. Print.

Yandell, Enid Bland. Lecture at the home of Mrs. Robert [Grace] McGann, Chicago. 11 Nov. 1915. Archives of American Art microfilm.

Zeiger, Susan. *In Uncle Sam's Service: Women Workers with the American Expeditionary Force, 1917–1919*. Ithaca, NY: Cornell UP, 1999. Print.

About the Editor

Writer-editor Elizabeth Foxwell's interest in women's contributions to World War I was sparked by the work of *Testament of Youth* author Vera Brittain; her Georgetown master's thesis on Brittain's World War II period received distinction. A specialist in the history of mystery/detective fiction and the recipient of Agatha and Dove awards, she lives outside of Washington, DC.

Learn more about U.S. women in the war on Foxwell's blog, "American Women in World War I," http://americanwomeninwwi.wordpress.com

CPSIA information can be obtained
at www.ICGtesting.com
Printed in the USA
LVOW08s1819120117
520748LV00005B/1178/P